GREAT LIFE
Great
MARRIAGE

God's "can't-miss" plan to understanding how the Kingdom
of God operates for success in every area of your life.

Don Griffin

LAURUS BOOKS

GREAT LIFE
Great
MARRIAGE

By Don Griffin

Paperback: ISBN: 978-1-938526-89-3

Mobi (Kindle): ISBN: 978-1-938526-90-9

ePub (iBooks, Nook): ISBN: 978-1-938526-91-6

Published by LAURUS BOOKS

LAURUS BOOKS
P.O. Box 530173
DeBary, Florida 32753-0173 USA
www.TheLaurusCompany.com

This book may be ordered in paperback from TheLaurusCompany.com,
Amazon.com, BarnesandNoble.com, and other retailers around the world. Also
available in formats for electronic readers from their respective stores.

Preface

As a teacher of God's Word and an occasional speaker for the past fifty years, I can truly say that the journey traveled, albeit with a few unnecessary detours, has been absolutely amazing. Allow me to share with you a few life-changing truths that have proven to be foundational to the great life and super fantastic marriage I have enjoyed. The first one is divinely simple, but in human terms, it is very complex, a type of paradox, if you will, and it is this: God's love is unconditional!

That God is love and therefore loves unconditionally is simple knowledge to the newest of Christians. But for me, it became very complex when I came to the realization that God knew, before He saved me, of the countless times I would be unfaithful to Him. Yet, in spite of this knowledge, He chose to save me. When I have been unfaithful to Him, more than seventy times seven, He has remained faithful and has done so because He had, and is still, completing a wonderful plan for my life. His plan included a great life and a great marriage that once seemed far beyond my grasp, but He extended His wonderful grace and caused it to become a reality. Conditional love could never cause that to happen because conditional love is a counterfeit of unconditional love. It is a mirage and is powerless to sustain itself.

GOOD NEWS!

God wants His unconditional love to become a reality in your heart as well because He wants all of His children to enjoy a great life that is inclusive of an ever-increasing, fun and wonderful marriage. Does this mean that all you have to do is push a button and, presto, everything changes? No, that is not the way His Kingdom operates. But as you receive more and more of His truth, knowledge, and understanding into your mind and heart, His best will become an overflowing river of abundance that will invigorate your soul and begin saturating every area of your life.

WARNING!!!

This is not a book about one giant leap for mankind, seven steps to better relationships, or ten steps to financial success. This book is about understanding how the Kingdom of God operates and gaining the knowledge necessary to be successful in every area of your life. Jesus went willingly to the Cross for the salvation of every soul, and if salvation alone was all that He accomplished, it would have been far more than the best sinner (there isn't one) could ever hope for. But He did far more. He made it possible for every born again believer to walk in continuous victory and enjoy life to the fullest, not just to endure it.

You may be a fan of books and teaching articles that set out a plan of action or teach self-discipline as a way of becoming successful, and if that is descriptive of you, I applaud your pursuit of excellence. There are several of those types of books in my library, and they do help, but you will never attain lasting success through your own work and effort. You may gain monetary success or be viewed as an important person by others, but none of the accolades bestowed by society have the power give you the peace, joy, harmony, and serendipities that accompany a Christ-centered life and marriage. Money can't do it, position can't do it, and education can't do it. The great life and great marriage you are seeking and searching for can only be obtained by letting God take control and allowing Him to change you from the inside out. No one, regardless of their sincerity, discipline, or dedication, can change from the outside in. Real and lasting change must take place from the inside out, and without the help of the Holy Spirit, it is an impossible task. With Him, all things are possible!

MORE GOOD NEWS!

The Holy Spirit is very patiently waiting and listening for you; waiting for you to ask, very pleased that you are seeking, and listening intently for your knock because then the doors to a great life and great marriage will be opened to you. He has given His word concerning these things, and God always keeps His word. God wants you to enjoy the great life and marriage He planned especially for you, even before you were conceived in your mother's womb.

Dear reader, I don't know your name or anything about you, but God knows your name, and He knows everything about you. Of this you can be certain, He created you to excel and succeed in every aspect of your life. He has numbered the hairs on your head and numbered your days to be long and prosperous, and through the Blood Atonement of Calvary, He made every provision that you will ever need to cause His will to come to pass in your life. God spoke through His prophet Jeremiah and said, *"'For I know the plans that I have for you,' declares the Lord, 'plans for welfare and not for calamity, to give you a future and a hope'"* (Jeremiah 29:11).

NEWS FLASH!!!

God hasn't changed His mind, and the too-good-to-be true-news is that His welfare is not the same as the welfare doled out by governments, however well meaning they may be. His welfare is supernatural in origin and predestined for every born-again believer. It contains an overflowing abundance of prosperity, financial and otherwise, for every part of life, and IS NOT, inclusive of calamity. Let's be in agreement that a new day has come, and the steady diet of debt, sickness, stress, and strife that have harassed you for so long is being erased forever. Enough of living in mediocrity. Let's come into agreement on that! Let's agree that you are taking possession of the "Great Life" and "Great Marriage" that God has appropriated and planned for all of His children. Let's also agree that all of His promises to you are "Yes" and "Amen" through Christ Jesus (see 2 Corinthians 1:20). "Amen," by the way, is not simply a word that ends a prayer; it is an affirmation that means, "It is so," or "It will be," in both Hebrew and Greek. It is speaking life into your prayer!

SUBMISSION IS THE BEGINNING

God wants you to know that as you begin this journey, the Holy Spirit is probably going to lead you out of your comfort zone. You can be certain that He will require you to be truthful with yourself and not allow any hidden rooms and closets to remain in your spiritual home. As you journey along, it's even possible that some of the traditions you have become enamored with over the years may come into question, questions like: "Does my tradition agree with Scripture," or, "Is my tradition putting limits on God?" The number of times tradition has impeded or even stopped God's children from receiving His best is staggering, but we can also agree that there are many good traditions. So take comfort, God is not on a vendetta of stamping out traditions that you love and hold dear unless they are burdensome and non-productive. Concerning some traditions that have the appearance of possessing spiritual value but are actually worthless, Jesus said, *"Neglecting the commandment of God, you hold to the traditions of men"* (Mark 7:8). What happens when you do that? Jesus answers this question in verse 13, *"... thus invalidating the word of God ..."*

Again, not all traditions are bad, and the Holy Spirit will never prompt you to make any changes that aren't best for you and your loved ones. However, some changes may be in order. He may ask you to examine the church you attend, and it's possible He could ask you to consider changing churches altogether. He may whisper in your spiritual ears that you need to change your inner circle of friends, or your job, but He will never ask you to leave anything unless He has something better.

Last, but not least, you can be comforted in knowing

that the Holy Spirit will never demand or force you to do anything. He will always leave the choices up to you. When changes do need to be made, He will supernaturally begin changing your heart, and His desires will become your desires. You will know when a season has ended. In perfect peace, you will be ready to move on with great anticipation to see what God has prepared for your future.

Dear reader, the very fact that you have this book in your hands is an affirmation that you truly do want more out of life, but wisdom says to carefully read and consider three very important questions before saying "yes" to this fun and exciting journey. Truth is never relative; it is always an absolute, so be true to yourself as you meditate and consider your answers.

1. *Are you ready to experience God's best and move into the supernatural where miracles and abundance are the norm?* Until you are, nothing in your life will really change.

2. *Are you ready to let God have control of all of your life?* That means every door of every room in your spiritual house must be open to Him. If it needs sweeping, you must be willing to let Him do the sweeping.

3. *Are you ready to let God remove every shackle, every chain, every encumbrance and begin walking in the Law of Liberty?*

If the answers are still, "Yes," let's pause for a moment and make special requests of our Father, knowing that it is His good pleasure to grant our desires.

PRAYER

"Heavenly Father, I thank You for physical eyes and ears, but I ask You now to give me spiritual eyes and spiritual ears so that I can receive all that You have for me. I ask You to illuminate my mind so that I can receive Your Word and gain a spiritual understanding of it as well. I realize that I can't change other people, but I can allow You, my Creator and Savior, to change me. I thank You in advance for what You are going to do in my life. In the name of Jesus, Your only Son, I pray. Amen."

If you could not pray that prayer because you are not a Christian, or perhaps you are not sure of your salvation, would you consider asking Jesus to come into your heart and forgive you of your sins? He is always faithful to do so, and you can be assured that there is no sin so big, no life too dirty, that He will not forgive and, by His blood that was shed at Calvary, wash away your sins forever, never to be remembered again. Don't wait. Ask Him now, and He will do it.

Contents

Chapter 1

As a Man Thinks, So Is He

Not everyone is familiar with the origin of the words found in this chapter title. It is a truth found in the Book of Proverbs that is simple, yet profound. These seven simple words are a stark reminder that your thought life, the way you think and even the way you process information, has brought you to the place in which you now find yourself. Some may argue that this is not an entirely true statement because circumstances, environment, and even luck (good or bad) had a part to play in this as well. While there may be mitigating factors, they don't alter the truth that your thought life has either caused you to overcome your circumstances and environment, or it has caused you to be held captive by them.

Here is another truth: If you really have a burning desire to change your present circumstances or environment, you can!

There are countless testimonies of people who once found themselves in dire situations due to upbringing, lack of education, etc., that went on to achieve great success in life. The reverse is also true, there are millions of people who have been blessed with the most advantageous of circumstances, yet success by almost any measure has eluded them completely. Therefore, with rare exception, we can agree that it's not your ethnicity that determines your future, but, ultimately, it's the way you think. As someone once said concerning finances, "Being broke is a temporary situation; being poor is a frame of mind." Incidentally, that holds true for every facet of your life.

It may seem that your circumstances and environment are the masters of your life, but God has both the will and the power to change everything that is wrong and replace it with everything that is right. How many times have you heard someone say, "That's just the way I am, and it's the way I will always be"? That kind of thinking is contrary to the Word of God and to the promises of God. He created you to be a winner, not to go through life in mediocrity. As to the matter of luck, the Bible gives no credibility to such a thing, and since the Word of God should be the foundation of every Christian's life, let's address this issue and then agree to once and forever take luck out of the equation.

Luck can easily be explained by preparation and opportunity, and it's interesting that the more prepared we are, the luckier we get. To be sure, there are games of chance, such as state lotteries, that appear to offer quick gain and success, but in reality they are games of deception. Proof of this is that most of the billboards advertising them are found in poor neighborhoods. For every perceived winner, there are hundreds and even thousands of losers. Participating in games of chance is more than poor stewardship; it is also a door opener that allows the enemy to erode one's faith to believe God as their total Provider. God is not pleased with a reckless steward.

THE MIND

Your mind and body are wonderful and complex creations of God, and depending on how you think, your mind will prove to be either your master or your servant. Consider that it takes just as much effort to think negatively as it does to think positively. Your mind has the power to make you a victor or a victim, a winner or a loser, a success or a failure, depending on how you have trained yourself to think. Your mind has the ability to see into the future, to reason and conceive, to believe or disbelieve. You can dream of future things and events and form mental images of them. You can create pictures and images of the person you want to marry or have already married. You can envision the home you want to live in, the lifestyle you want to live, the vacations you want to take, and any other thing you want your mind to visualize by simply commanding it to do so. But the key to winning the battle that rages in the mind is not about one's IQ. It's about thinking with the mind of Christ.

Yet, here is the difficulty: only men and women who train their minds to be their servants will enjoy true peace and see their God-given goals and dreams birthed into reality. When this is the case, you will be reminded of certain Kingdom truths and how the Kingdom operates over and over again as you move from chapter to chapter. Repetition is a very necessary part of renewing your mind.

THE HEART OF THE MATTER

Where does your mind receive its resources? They come from your heart. Your heart is your mind's library, or in the modern vernacular, your hard drive. Your mind records what it has seen and heard and dutifully stores the information in your heart. Your entire life is stored there and is awaiting the command to produce what you ask it to produce. You can tell it to produce a picture of an elephant because you have seen an elephant. You can visualize things in nature because you have seen them before. Therefore, it is of vital importance to understand that your mind doesn't care what you allow it to receive. Its job is simply to receive and store whatever you choose to allow to come in. What's currently stored in your heart is the reason you think the way you do.

Let's press on from the physical realm and begin pressing into the spiritual or supernatural realm, where all battles are won and lost. Unlike Old Covenant saints whose hearts were governed by the Laws of Moses that produced judgment and condemnation, the New Covenant that Christ provided for His Church has given you a complete heart transplant and made it possible for you to live free of past failures, regrets, and condemnation because you now live under the Law of Liberty.

What is the Law of Liberty? Jesus told the Church with great simplicity how the New Law of Liberty operates when He said, *"You shall love the Lord your God with all your heart, … your soul, and … your mind"* (Matthew 22:37). That a new and better covenant was necessary is evidenced by the Cross. The Law was powerless to remove sin and therefore powerless to save, but that doesn't mean that the

16

Old Covenant was a failure. No, the Law written in stone was holy, and it accomplished everything God designed it to do. It revealed to Israel that they were sinners who desperately needed a Savior, and it still sends the same message today to a lost and dying world, *"realizing the fact that law is not made for a righteous person, but for those who are lawless ..."* (unsaved / 1 Timothy 1:9). The New Covenant has replaced the Old, and the two Covenants—Law and Grace—are not to be mixed. Jesus confirmed that these are not to be mixed when he said, *"Nor do people put new wine into old wineskins ..."* (Matthew 9:17). When we make Jesus our first love, the Old Covenant of works is swallowed up by Grace.

As you train your mind to focus and adhere to the New Law of Liberty, God will empower you to effortlessly keep the Old Testament laws that once governed and controlled your life. It bears repeating, you are no longer under the Law. You are now immersed in Grace, and while it is no longer a necessity to keep the Old Testament Law to keep us seated in heavenly places with Jesus, the laws that govern love and morality are unchanging. An appropriate analogy would be to compare a Christian to an apple tree. An apple tree doesn't produce apples because it decides to, it produces apples because that is what it was created to do. It's the same with you. You are able to love others and live a life that is pleasing to God because He lives in you. As this truth becomes more dominant in your thought life, your mentality of trying to please God and people through works will take on an entirely new perspective. The apostle Paul reminded the saints at Philippi, *"and the peace of God, which surpasses all understanding, will guard your hearts and minds through Christ Jesus"* (Philippians 4:7 NKJV). Your soul person will enjoy more and more rest and peace as you cease from trying to make yourself a better person and begin immersing yourself in the finished work of the Cross. Enjoying God's peace and rest is an essential element of enjoying a great life and a great marriage.

As a born-again believer in Jesus Christ, you are now a new creation with a new heart that has an intuitive desire to seek God and the things of God. The inner voice of your spirit man is constantly speaking to your mind in an effort to lead, guide, and direct your daily walk and decisions. However, it is possible to miss His voice completely unless you are tuned in to His channel. The world has its own broadcast station and is constantly competing for your mind's attention. Even so, Satan is not God and isn't nearly as powerful and cunning as he would have you believe. The truth of the matter is that he is powerless to hurt you in any way unless you allow him to take root in your mind and contaminate your belief system.

God is omniscient (all-knowing), omnipotent (all-powerful), and omnipresent (always present), not lacking in anything, while Satan has none of those characteristics. Therefore, he does not know what you are thinking unless you speak your thoughts aloud. So, what does he do? He throws darts at your mind and then closely watches your reactions while listening intently to your words. Remember, there are evil thoughts, and there are thoughts of evil. He will attempt to send you evil and discouraging thoughts, but you have been empowered to cast them down and reject his attempts to master your thought life.

For this reason, Jesus said, "LISTEN *TO THIS!*" (Mark

4:3). Jesus began His parable of the sower with these words and then later explained to His disciples that the words you speak are seeds that give birth to life or death (much more on this subject later). He concludes the parable by saying, "... *Take care what you listen to* ..." (Mark 4:24). Jesus was reminding us of the great importance of monitoring what you see and hear and of learning to recognize His voice.

THE INNER CIRCLE

Who you spend time with is of tremendous importance. Spending time with the wrong people is a major infectious culprit that causes countless numbers of Christians to live lives that fall far short of God's best. Those individuals you allow into your inner circle, and your friends in general, have already played a vital role in helping or hindering your quest for a great life and marriage, and they will continue to do so. When you spend time with people who rarely, or worse—never, talk about spiritual things, you would do well to pray and evaluate the effect they are having on you. You should also be cautious of those who, although they may talk about spiritual things, fail to reflect in their lives the joy and success you are striving for. That doesn't mean that you have to exclude them from your life, but it may be wise to spend less time with them and strongly consider excluding them from your inner circle.

As promised, we will look at the power of spoken words in greater detail as we continue our journey, but suffice it to say that the people you choose to spend time with are constantly lifting you up or pulling you down, depending on their attitudes and words. Someone correctly said, "Small minds talk about problems and gossip about other people; average minds talk about the weather and current events; while great minds talk about the Kingdom, about the goodness of God, and of the dreams and goals He has placed into their hearts. God is no respecter of persons. He is waiting with a patient ear for you to ask and is more than willing to lead you into the wonderful future that He has planned for your life.

Another inner circle of friends you must constantly evaluate does not consist of real people in the true sense of the word, but they do have a voice and wield a great deal of influence in your life. Who are these people? They appear on iPads, cell phones, Facebook, and other social media, magazines, blogs, television programs, and movies. You must be wise and exercise as much discernment in this area of your life as you do in your close and intimate friendships. They really are a part of your inner circle and are constantly spewing information into your mind. The world wants to use these devices to shape your family values and control the way you think and live, but God's Word reminds us, *"Do not be deceived: 'Bad company corrupts good morals'"* (1 Corinthians 15:33). Consider that under the guidance of the Holy Spirit, your mind has the ability to separate good and evil, but your flesh left unguarded is never a match for temptation.

Everyone, even born-again Christians, possess a flesh that desires to have a great love affair with the world, but it can only hurt and deceive you when you allow it to dethrone the Spirit. That is why the apostle Paul said, *"I discipline* [Lit *bruise*] *my body and make it my slave ..."* (1 Corinthians 9:27). That is pretty severe! As you begin to make a conscious effort to say no to your flesh, the battles will become less numerous and easier to win, but as long as you live in a fleshly body, you must always be on guard. Your enemy will attempt to use your flesh as a tool to bring compromise and confusion, but that is never true of the Holy Spirit who lives inside of you. He is never confused and is never the author of confusion. He can easily discern light from darkness, evil from good, and truth from lies. His voice is always speaking in an attempt to correct and direct your path by gently saying words, such as, "No, don't do this," or "Don't talk like that. That's not who you are; that's who you were."

The Holy Spirit is always standing guard in an effort to keep bad information from gaining ground in your mind. He knows that the enemy is constantly looking for a pathway into your heart, and in times of crisis, double mindedness will very likely result, creating a lack of faith and a lack of direction. Continued doses of negative input will allow a spiritual disease called "hardness of heart" to afflict both your mind and your physical body. When this is not corrected by spending time in the Word and prayer, the voice of the Holy Spirit will become difficult to hear, but this is never because God isn't speaking. The voice of the Holy Spirit is transmitting 24/7, but too much worldly interference can make it difficult to hear Him.

There is a reason that God commanded Adam not to eat of the tree of good and evil. He knew that doing so would bring death to Adam, and it will do the same thing to you. Satan's tactics remain the same. He is looking for Christians who are double minded from continually mixing worldly wisdom with the wisdom of God. He knows that a double-minded person is easy to confuse and control, so he is relentless in his mission to take ground that doesn't belong to him. Once he finds open doors to access your mind, he can immediately begin building strongholds that have the power to enslave and control your life.

TIME TO PONDER

Let's put our journey on pause for a moment and consider a few pertinent questions.

1. What is the Holy Spirit saying about your inner circle?

2. Do you have a tendency to think in the positive, or the negative?

3. Do you really believe that your life can and will change for the better?

4. Do you get up each day with excitement and anticipation of good things, or do you find yourself getting up with an attitude that says, "Another day of the same old same old"?

5. Do you see yourself living in abundance, or lack; of more than enough, or hoping you can get by; healthy, or sick?

6. Are you at perfect peace, or is there a constant nagging in your heart that causes you to fear and worry?

7. Do you laugh and smile a lot, or, if honest, would you have to confess that you seldom laugh and, when you do, most of your smiles are designed to hide your real emotions?

It's grade time! But take heart, God always grades on a winning curve, and with Him, it's impossible to fail!

If you see yourself in the column of positive Word thinkers, then you have a head start in moving on to a much higher level, the supernatural level, where favor and abundance are overflowing from the Kingdom of God. If, however, you admit to being prone to worry and find yourself dwelling on negative thoughts, then you aren't where you need to be. But be encouraged, your mind is already beginning the process of being reprogramed, *"for it is God who is at work in you, both to will and to work for His good pleasure"* (Philippians 2:13).

Whichever column you currently see yourself in is because of the way your heart and mind are currently programmed. But be of good cheer, no one has arrived. Take heart in the fact that you are no longer at the starting gate and that you have already embarked on the Emmaus Road that leads to a great life and a supernaturally great marriage. Life is a continuous journey and full of seasons.

Here is the almost too good to be true news that God is shouting from heaven: He has a simple, can't-miss program for helping you live the abundant life (John 10:10). Remember, it's not about trying to think positive in an effort to become a better Christian or a better person. It's not about better church attendance or reading your Bible more. It has nothing to do with your doing anything. It has everything to do with what Christ has done and allowing Him to work through you. It's about training yourself to think with the Mind of Christ (1 Corinthians 2:16).

In Romans 12:2, God gives tremendous insight into how all born-again Christians can train themselves to think as Christ thinks, *"And be not conformed to this world: but be ye* [that's you] *transformed by the renewing of your mind ..."* (KJV). Please note that this is not a suggestion; it's a command. But it's a command that most Christians have not understood and, consequently, have done a poor job of implementing into their lives.

Notice that there are two directives.

THE FIRST DIRECTIVE:

"Do not be conformed to this world."

How are you conformed to this world? By thinking like the world thinks. If you think as the world thinks, then you will most certainly find yourself being conformed to it. Unfortunately, after receiving salvation, an alarming number of Christians fail to renew their minds with the Word, and the results are obvious. The Church at large still tends to think in much the same way that the world thinks, and unwittingly finds itself living and thinking in much the same way as the unsaved world.

For instance, born-again believers who have trusted in Christ should not continue to see banks as their primary money source and doctors as their primary healing source. There isn't anything sinful or sinister about banks or doctors, but they aren't God's best. We will take a closer and more in depth look at how God's Kingdom operates later on, but for now, allow this seed of knowledge to take root in your heart: *"It is better to take refuge in the Lord than to trust in man"* (Psalm 118:8). It's no coincidence that this Scripture is the centerpiece of all Scripture.

Let me add a word of caution: Don't read this and become foolish about your level of faith! God will always meet you at your point of faith, but wishing and hoping is not faith. Instead, believing that it's impossible for God's promises to fail is faith. Until your faith is up to it, Jesus is more than willing for you to see doctors and use medicines, and He won't love you more or less when you do. Regardless of the method, there is no healing apart from the Great Physician, Jesus, and He wants you to be well and prosperous.

TWO WISDOMS

The world's wisdom says same-sex marriage, live-in partners, and abortions on demand are normal and acceptable in the new age in which we live, but God is not in agreement with their opinion. Our God is the God of the Ages and is unmoved by political correctness. The world's wisdom tries to adjust God's moral boundaries by either ignoring or changing His Word to accommodate its own standards of morality, but God is unchanging. Make no mistake about it, there is an evil and sinister spirit working overtime, 24/7, with the goal of capturing your mind, controlling the way you think, and conforming you to this world. Yet, you can take a moment to praise God, the Almighty One, for *"... greater is He who is in you than he who is in the world"* (1 John 4:4).

THE SECOND DIRECTIVE:

"Be ye transformed by the renewing of your mind."

One definition of "transformed" found in Webster's is: "To change something or someone completely, usually in a good way." Let's bear in mind that God's command to be transformed is directed to His children, not those who belong to the world. Sadly, non-believers can't change themselves, and in the flesh, neither can the Believer. But you are not of the flesh, for you have been born of the Spirit of God. The moment you received Christ as your Savior, your spirit person was made alive and is absolutely complete because it is the same Holy Spirit living in you that raised Jesus Christ from the dead (Romans 8:11). That is not true of your physical body, even though it is the temple that houses your heart, mind, and soul.

The Apostle Paul recognized that we are all a continuous work in progress under the inspiration of the Holy Spirit when he proclaimed, *"… He who began a good work in you will perfect it until the day of Christ Jesus"* (Philippians 1:6). And that, dear reader, is what He is now doing with you at this very moment. Hold fast to this truth as you continue to progress through this book in your quest for a great life and a great marriage: Every Christian has been placed on the Potter's wheel, and God is the Potter. What a grand and glorious place to be, firmly in the hands of the Potter. As the wheel turns in His hands, every blemish, every hurt, and every discouragement that would keep you from being complete and perfected is being removed. Proverbs 25:4 says, *"Take away the dross from the silver, and there comes out a vessel for the smith."* Even now, at this very moment, the Holy Spirit is gently removing the dross as He speaks and renews your mind. His purpose is to lead, guide, and direct you into the fullness of God's plan and purpose for your life.

CARNAL MINDEDNESS

We won't take a lot of time on this subject for now, but as we come to the end of this chapter and continue our journey, it's important for us to touch on the subject of carnal-mindedness so that you can begin to gain a better understanding of what it is and is not. Most Christians believe that a carnal mind is synonymous with sinful thoughts, but that is not really true. However, please be warned, to continually think with a carnal mind will, in time, lead to sin. All non-believers are carnally minded, but a born-again believer can also be carnally minded.

WHAT IS A CARNAL MIND?

A carnal mind is one that is driven, motivated, and controlled by the flesh with its five senses of touch, taste, smell, hearing, and sight, and by the wisdom of the world. Does this mean that your five senses are evil? No, in fact they are necessary and wonderful gifts from your Creator that allow you to live and enjoy your physical life here on earth. With them you can enjoy the touch and caress of a loved one while relishing the smell and scent of fragrant perfumes and flowers. You can have your senses enticed by the inviting smell of food being prepared. Your ears can hear the sounds of nature and animals as well as discern spoken words that allow you to communicate at the highest level of life. You can see the beauty of nature, of breathtaking views of blue ocean water sending white foaming waves crashing onto rocks as they exhaust themselves on white sandy beaches. Surrounded by darkness, you can gaze thousands of miles into the sky and enjoy the beauty of the stars spoken into existence by your loving Father. To be sure, these are good gifts, and it is important to receive the real truth contained in the gospels that God only gives good things to His children (see James 1:16-17). As wonderful and useful as your five physical senses are, it's important to realize that mature Christians don't allow their physical senses and emotions to control them. Mature Christians are those who have trained their senses to be under the control of the indwelling Holy Spirit.

As you can see, your mind is where the battles of life are now being fought. It is there that your quest for a successful future will be won or lost. Even so, God won the spiritual battle at the Cross that entitles you to a great life and a great marriage, and the spiritual always triumphs over the physical. It is because of His great and resounding victory that you can now "*... reign in life through the One, Jesus Christ*" (Romans 5:17).

"As a man thinks, so is he!"

Chapter 2
Let's Check Your ID

I t's time for an ID checkup, not so others will know who you are, but to affirm to yourself who you are. In the perilous days in which we now live, it is imperative for you to be sure of your true spiritual identification. Man's inhumanity to man is becoming more evil and violent with each passing day, while the entire earth groans and belches ever louder. Yes, something is about to happen, but you can take solace that the One who will cause every prophecy to come about exactly as He said also holds your future.

Old Testament prophets told of a coming Messiah to the nation of Israel who would die and make full atonement for the sins of the world. That prophecy was fulfilled in God's only begotten Son, Jesus. They prophesied that Israel would cease to be a nation, and its people would be scattered over the face of the earth. That prophecy has been fulfilled. They prophesied that in the Last Days (dispensation of time following the Cross), God would, in one day, rebirth the nation of Israel. That prophecy was fulfilled in 1948. The prophet Joel prophesied that God's covenant people would be gathered once again into the land He blessed and gave them as a reward to Abrahams's seed, Isaac and Jacob. Joel's prophecy is currently being fulfilled as Jews from all over the world flow daily into the land of Israel.

Jesus, the Son of God and the greatest of all the prophets, told His disciples of His coming death and resurrection; He completed that prophecy two thousand years ago. He also prophesied that He would one day return to rule and reign here on earth. That prophecy is the hope of the Church, and the fulfillment is close at hand. Jesus said of His second coming, *"Unless those days had been cut short, no life would have been saved; but for the sake of the elect those days will be cut short"* (Matthew 24:22). The seven years preceding the return of Christ, especially the last three and a half years, will be a type of hell on earth, but Jesus will have the final say and record the final victory. The Anti-Christ and False Prophet will be defeated and cast into the Lake of Fire. Satan will be bound in chains, and Christ will rule and reign with His saints (you are one) for a thousand years, and then comes the judgment.

Undeniably, the end is near, and all around us, it seems that evil is winning. But "be of good cheer" (see John 16:33), for nothing could be farther from the truth!

To be sure, God doesn't want you walking around with your head in the sand, but neither does He want you to worry and travail about the future. Compared to all other times in history when you could have lived, the current Church age exceeds them all. It is a great time to raise children, enjoy the fruit of your labor, and accomplish the wonderful plan that God has established for your life. It is not a time to wring your hands and be fearful. Rather, it's a time to raise your hands and shout, "Thank You, Lord, for victory!"

Peter said, *"Grace and peace be multiplied to you in the knowledge of God and of Jesus our Lord"* (2 Peter 1:2). For a small segment of the Church, grace and peace is being multiplied, but for the greater part of the Church, it is apparent that a supernatural understanding of its real identity in Christ needs to take place. That knowledge, and that knowledge alone, will enable the Church to live victoriously in perilous times. Please understand that when I use the word "Church," I'm speaking of the *ekklesia*, the called out body of Christ, not the brick and mortar local buildings where they gather.

That is the purpose and goal of this chapter, to help you understand your true identity. The enemy has been very successful in keeping a large segment of the Church confused about its true identity, especially the Christians who live in America. That is beginning to change, however, as light overtakes darkness. For now, let's narrow our focus to you and look into three key areas of knowledge where God is bringing fresh revelation. As the unveiling begins to take place, the Holy Spirit will open your spiritual eyes and allow you to receive spiritual insight that will enable you to live in greater victory and freedom than ever before. He is holding nothing back.

THREE KEYS

1. You must know who you are in Christ.
2. You must understand the finished work that Jesus accomplished on the Cross.
3. You must carry your ID with you at all times.

THE SEAL IS BROKEN

God commanded His prophet Daniel to, "... *seal up the book until the end of time; many will go back and forth, and knowledge will increase*" (Daniel 12:4).

IN THE SPIRITUAL

As you read and meditate on this wonderful prophecy, it's easy to see and understand that God wasn't talking about technology alone. Instead, He was prophesying about something of much greater importance. The prophecy centers on the coming Messiah and the mystery of the ages; the Christian Church. Daniel prophesied that His Church would be birthed by the power of the Cross, the blood of Christ, and His resurrection. Has it taken place? Yes! In fact, it happened exactly as God said it would, and since the birth of the Christian Church, there has been an absolute explosion of souls being saved around the entire world. The evidence in the spiritual ream is overwhelming, but it was also necessary for an explosion of new knowledge to take place in the physical realm, and that has happened as well.

IN THE PHYSICAL

New technology is being birthed at an astounding rate. Technology that was new only ten years ago is almost immediately replaced with even newer and more efficient technology with such rapidity that change has become the norm. Most of the gadgets and commodities that make life easier and more luxurious today were inconceivable and far-fetched only two hundred years ago. This is truly amazing when we consider that mankind lived and traveled with virtually no improvements for almost seven thousand years. The harnessing of electricity, the light bulb, automobiles, airplanes, steam engines, computers, and cell phones are but a few of the modern marvels that were waiting for God to remove the seal. All of the resources necessary to bring these life-changing inventions into existence had always existed, but God, in His sovereignty, kept this knowledge sealed until now. Why now? To usher in and bring to completion His prophetic plan concerning the "End Time" that must take place before the return of Christ to earth.

THE WAR FOR YOUR FUTURE

The worldwide technology explosion taking place is quite evident and easily seen, but there is an even greater explosion going on in the spiritual world that can't be seen. The war between good and evil is intensifying because Satan realizes that the return of Christ is imminent. He knows he can't control your eternal destination because your life has been sealed in Christ, but he also knows that if he can keep you from knowing your true identity, you will live your life far below the best that Jesus purchased for you at Calvary. In short, you will never be able to obtain the desires your Creator has placed into your heart, and you will be a very small threat to the kingdom of darkness.

The psalmist declared, "Delight yourself also in the LORD, and He shall give you the desires of your heart" (Psalm 37:4).

As you read and meditate on God's promise to give you the desires of your heart, ask yourself the following four questions:

1. What are the desires of my heart?
2. Are they clearly defined?
3. Can I articulate them to myself and others?
4. Are they large enough that they can't be reached or obtained without the help of the Almighty?

Someone once said, "A person without a dream will always go back to their past, but a person with a dream will leave their past and eagerly seek the future." If now is not the time to release your faith and grab hold of your God-given dreams and desires, then when?

You know that all of God's promises are true, but do you really believe that His promises will prove to be a reality in your life? Is there a voice that says, "I know He can, but I am not absolutely sure that He will?" If you find those negative thoughts successfully attacking your mind, God wants you to know that you aren't alone. An extraordinary number of born-again Christians have the same self-defeating doubts, and they have them because they don't understand their true identity in Christ.

For this reason, it's time to cut to the chase and reveal what the kingdom of darkness does not want you to know, and that is who God says that you are. Jesus warned that Satan's mission is "*... to steal and kill and destroy ...*" (John 10:10), and his mission will never change. His relentless mission of stealing (health, prosperity, joy, and content-ment), killing (dreams and goals), and destroying (lives, marriages, relationships) is relatively easy to accomplish in the lives of Christians who don't know their true identity. That is why God wants His children to see themselves as triumphant joint heirs of the Kingdom of God, not unworthy and undeserving sinners.

SHOW YOUR ID

In today's society, it's almost impossible to travel, drive a car, or engage in buying or selling without proper identification. You must be able to prove you are who you claim to be. Your ID must have certain information, such as name, date of birth, and sex. It's an even greater confidence builder when your picture is embossed on your ID, further proving that you are who you claim to be. If that is true of the physical world we live in, and it is, how much greater is the importance of possessing the proper ID that will allow you to access the fullness of God's Kingdom in the spirit realm.

You are probably familiar with the Sermon on the Mount when Jesus preached to a multitude of people and said, *"But seek ye first the kingdom of God, and his righteousness; and all these things shall be added unto you,"* (Matthew 6:33 KJV). But are you aware that when you made Jesus the Lord and Savior of your life, He *"... qualified us* [you] *to share in the inheritance of the saints in Light. For He rescued us* [you] *from the domain* [authority] *of darkness, and transferred us* [you] *to the Kingdom of His beloved Son"* (Colossians 1:12-13 bracketed words added for clarity).

It is imperative that you understand these life-changing truths because the average Christian will live their entire life "seeking the Kingdom" when, spiritually speaking, they are already "of the Kingdom." The miracle of the Cross was still future when Jesus first gave this command to seek the Kingdom, but now you can look back and see the triumphant victory of the Cross and revel in the knowledge that everything Jesus came to earth to do has been accomplished. When Christ returns to earth, all of His children will actually

35

be "in the Kingdom" that He prayed and requested of His Father to take place. But you already have full access and ownership of all of God's spiritual Kingdom resources in the here and now. While we should never stop seeking for more and more of Jesus, it's time for God's children to stop asking Him for what He has already given us.

Let me encourage you to reread and meditate on the verses of scripture related to His Kingdom. As Light begins to come and darkness begins to fade, command your mind to show you a clear, blemish-free mirror with your reflection on it. As you gaze at the person in the mirror, are you as absolutely confident of your spiritual ID as you are of your physical ID? Do you see someone who is free and victorious, or do you see someone bound and unsure of their future?

Yes _____   No _____

Somewhat _____   Don't understand _____

If someone were to ask you to identify yourself and prove that you are a Christian, what would you say? Someone once said, "I'm not who you think I am. I'm not even who I think I am. I have become the person that others think I am." With that in mind, what type of picture do you imagine would depict your actual appearance as a child of God? Even more importantly, how do you think God sees you?

You can probably point to a time in your life when you were saved and baptized. You probably remember the person who led you to Christ. You can probably recite those times and places. But years later, the average Christian still does not comprehend what happened when their salvation took place. One of the most popular terms Christians use in an attempt to tell others who they are in Christ is, "I'm just an old sinner saved by grace," or "I'm an undeserving child of God." That is an absolutely true description of every lost soul before their salvation experience, but what does God say about His children after salvation?

Years of teaching and interacting with Christians of many different denominations have confirmed that most believers still see themselves as sinners and undeserving to receive anything from God. Why is this deception so prevalent? Once again, it's largely due to wrong teaching and preaching that conveys the message that God is still judging the Church based on performance and obedience. The end result is a sin-consciousness that corrodes one's Christian faith. That mindset makes it almost impossible to receive God's invitation to enter boldly into the throne room of grace and make requests with any significant measure of expectation that God will answer.

Allow me to share a recent but, unfortunately, all too common example of the great harm that results from mixing the Old Covenant of Law with the New Covenant of Grace.

I was asked by a friend to accompany him to witness and pray for a middle-aged man who had been diagnosed with cancer. The doctors told him that the disease had spread throughout his body and that he had only a short time to live. He was a farmer by vocation and very prosperous, but there can come a time when the amount of money and fortune one has amassed really doesn't mean anything. The only thing that will matter is our relationship with Jesus. I asked him if he was sure of his salvation, and he replied that he was. I then asked him if he knew that God wanted him healed, and he replied, "I know that He can if it's His will and if I work hard enough." I replied, "Mr. Frank, how hard did you have to work to get saved?" He responded, "I didn't." I asked again, "If you couldn't work hard enough to get saved, then why do you think you can work hard enough to get healed?" We prayed and believed God would heal him of his cancer. It's a done deal when faith meets faith that is full of good expectations, but it is very often an uphill battle when the sick person sees their relationship with God as being performance based.

Do you see? That type of thinking will always produce a mindset of sin-consciousness and condemnation that chokes the healing power of God and a true understanding of grace. Obviously, how you see yourself after salvation won't keep you out of heaven, but that is future, and God wants you to enjoy a great life and great marriage in the here and now. Living in sickness, financial lack, and emotional stress is not God's plan for your life, and He is not causing those things to happen to teach you something. While that may be a prevalent misunderstanding of many denominations today, it is not God's will for your life. How you see yourself will translate into how you see life. Just as importantly, how you think that God sees you will be the deciding factor that leads you into victory, mediocrity, or utter loss. Therefore, let's allow God's Word to enlighten your mind, remembering always, *"As a man thinks, so is he."*

LET'S START AT "THE BEGINNING"

Let's get this straight. Man did not create himself, and neither did man evolve from a type of archaic homo sapien that somehow emerged from the sea, and over a period of millions of years eventually evolved into the person you now see in the mirror. When you look at an elegant watch that has been engineered to keep the precise time and date, you would never think that, given some inordinate amount of time, it somehow evolved itself into existence. Even if time were increased to millions or even billions of years, you would never believe that somehow, someway, by chance and chance alone, all of the parts to make that watch into a complete and beautiful timepiece somehow evolved into being, and then put itself together. Not even so-called atheists would ever accept as fact that a watch could somehow evolve into being.

What then could we all agree upon? How did the watch come into existence? We can all agree that the watch was created by a person with a superior mind with superior skills that we might refer to as a "Master Craftsman." In the same way, man, who is far more complex than a watch, was created by the hands of a Master Craftsman for the purpose of glorifying his Creator and ruling and reigning in this life (see Genesis 1:28). That is a truth much greater than the theory of evolution! Man can now use the resources at his disposal to create useful and beautiful things because the seal of knowledge has been broken, but not even the most brilliant mind or any earthly power can create life from nothing. Only God can create life, and He did. The psalmist declared, "... *for I am fearfully and wonderfully made*" (Psalm 139:14).

GOD ALWAYS KEEPS HIS WORD

If you have never taken time to read the biblical account of the first five days of creation, I would encourage you to do so, but let's read together what happened on the sixth day. On the sixth day, God said, *"Let Us* [Father, Son, Holy Spirit] *make man in Our image, according to Our likeness; and let them rule over the fish of the sea and over the birds of the sky and over the cattle and over all the earth, and over every creeping thing that creeps on the earth"* (Genesis 1:26 bracketed words added for clarity). Did He do it? Yes, He did it because God cannot lie, and He is always faithful to watch over His Word to perform it. Verse 27, *"God created man in His own image, in the image of God He created Him; male and female He created them."* Verse 28, *"God blessed them ..."*

You don't want to miss what happened. God is Spirit, and He is also triune, so He created Adam and Eve as triune beings of spirit, soul, and body. The Bible records, *"Then the LORD God ... breathed into his nostrils the breath of life; and man became a living being"* (Genesis 2:7). God is pure, holy, and sinless, and He created Adam and Eve the same way—pure, holy, and untainted by sin.

This warrants repeating. God created them spirit, soul, and body, and they were sinless. They were not created with a sin nature, and death was never a part of God's plan for them. They were created to live forever, with their spirit person having complete rule and dominion over their minds. This allowed them to communicate with God at the very highest level of knowledge and understanding. In other words, they didn't need a High Priest to mediate on their behalf because they had the standing of a High Priest.

The door to their Creator was always open, and the welcome mat was always out. In essence, although they were not Christ, they were sinless and had the mind of Christ. To complete the picture, God then placed them in a beautiful and lush land called "The Garden of Eden."

What a grand place to be. They had an ironclad covenant with God that guaranteed they would never be sick, never be in debt, and never have any worries or tribulations. To add icing to the cake in terms we can understand, God gave them legal power of attorney to rule and reign over all the earth. Does that mean God gave up His sovereignty? No, God is sovereign and always will be, but He did transfer legal authority to Adam and commanded him to use this authority to rule and reign over the entire earth. The psalmist said it this way: *"The heavens are the heavens of the LORD, but the earth He has given to the sons of men"* (Psalm 115:16). The only thing that could cause them to lose their authority and make their covenant with God null and void would be if they chose to disobey the command He gave to Adam: *"... From any tree of the garden you may eat freely; but from the tree of the knowledge of good and evil you shall not eat, for in the day you eat from it you will surely die"* (Genesis 2:16-17).

TRIALS AND TEMPTATIONS

Adam had an adversary whose mission was to destroy him and steal the power of attorney with which God had entrusted him. Adam's enemy was a fallen angel named Satan, and you have the same adversary! While this may be Bible 101 to most readers, God did not create Satan in his present form. God created a magnificent cherub angel that

He named Lucifer, and He created him for a purpose. This purpose was to send him to earth as a protector and covering, to watch over Adam and the earth and to respond to Adam's beck and call (Ezekiel 28:14). But what happened? In the same way that God created Adam and Eve with the freedom to make choices, He also created angels with this same ability, and Lucifer made a bad choice of colossal proportions.

The prophet Isaiah describes Lucifer as being one of the most powerful and most beautiful of all the angels that God had ever created, but Lucifer blew it all when he said, *"... I will ascend to heaven; I will raise my throne above the stars of God ... I will make myself like the Most High"* (Isaiah 14:13-14). The moment Lucifer rebelled, His identity changed, and his once exalted name of "Lucifer" became synonymous with Satan, known throughout the heavens and on earth as the Serpent and the Old Dragon. He was enraged at God because he no longer had a place in God's heavenly kingdom, so he immediately embarked on a mission to become the ruler over all the heavens that surround earth, and of earth itself. He would use all of his sinister power and skills to "steal, kill, and destroy" the man created by the hands of God, Adam.

The Temptation

We are all familiar with what happened next. The serpent (Satan) appeared to Eve with a first edition of "Better Homes and Gardens" because he knew that the only way to steal their authority was to deceive them into doing the one thing God had commanded them not to do. Dear reader, his tactics have never changed. Disobedience is always the root that leads to death, and Satan knew that the only way to establish this root was through one of these three temptations; *"... the lust of the flesh, the lust of the eyes, and the pride of life ..."* (1 John 2:16). It is worth pointing out that this verse continues and shows the root of these temptations, *"... is not from the Father, but is from the world."* All other sins such as envy, anger, strife, unforgiveness, and hatred are the bitter fruit that begins to manifest itself as a result of giving in to any of these three worldly temptations.

Let's listen in on their conversation because it's the same conversation Satan wants to have with anyone foolish enough to talk with him.

The serpent asked in Genesis 3:1, *"Indeed, has God said, 'You shall not eat from any tree of the garden'?"* Get the gist? He knew what God had said, so he proceeded to appeal to her flesh. And how did Eve respond? *"From the fruit of the trees of the garden we may eat; but from the fruit of the tree which is in the middle of the garden, God has said, 'You shall not eat from it or touch it, or you will die'"* (Genesis 3:2-3).

Here is a valuable lesson to learn in your quest to enjoy a great life and a great marriage, and that is to know and study God's Word. Missing His truths by just a little gives the enemy the ability to extract a lot. This is what happened to Eve. Although God did command them not to eat of the tree in the middle of the garden, He never said, "Don't touch it." Now, would it be wise to tempt yourself by touching something that you know is off limits? The answer of course is "No" because whatever you set your mind on will, in time, become the object of your desires and confessions, and that can be good or bad. In this case it was bad to the nth degree.

Satan's first temptation came to Eve in the form of a suggestion that appealed to her flesh, and he had a great measure of success in this area. Next, he offered temptation number two and appealed to the lust of the eyes. Jesus called Satan the "father of lies," and with good reason, because he now tells her the first lie recorded in the Bible, one that still reverberates through the ages. He said to Eve, "... *You surely will not die*"(Genesis 3:4). Have you ever noticed that a lie can never stand by itself, that it always requires more lies as it attempts to cover and hide itself? So Satan follows up lie number one with lie number two, "*For God knows that in the day you eat from it your eyes will be opened, and you will be like God* [pride of life], *knowing good and evil*" (Genesis 3:5 bracketed words added).

Satan had now tempted Eve with all three temptations with full knowledge that once she took the bait, both she and Adam would lose their covenant with God. With the covenant no longer in place, their power of attorney would then belong to him, and he would become the prince and power of this heaven and this earth (Ephesians 2:1). What happened? "... *the woman saw that the tree was good for food, and that it was a delight to the eyes, and that the tree was desirable to make one wise ...*"(Genesis 3:6). Again, let's keep the record straight! The Bible faithfully recorded what Eve saw, but what she saw was not the truth concerning what God had said. What she saw and chose to believe was a total lie sold to her by the father of lies, Satan. Sadly, all of this could have been avoided had Adam not abdicated his position as head of the home.

How about you? When trials and temptations come as

they did to Adam and Eve, how do you respond? Mr. Adam, are you on guard? Do you know the condition of your flock (Proverbs 27:23)? Mrs. Eve, are you tuned in to the voice of God? Are you in a state of contentment and at rest in the Lord? Everyone at various times will find themselves tempted in much the same way that Adam and Eve were tempted, and here is a revelation concerning any temptation: No one, not Satan, not any spirit, nor any person can force anyone to sin. Everyone sins because of wrong thinking and wrong believing. Sin is conceived when, despite having received Light, you make a conscious choice to give in to the deception and choose to sin. On the other hand, even though you may at times stumble and fall short when temptation comes, if you no longer desire to sin, then a heart transplant has taken place, and the new you has a heart that is very desirous of pleasing Jesus.

THE TRUTH ABOUT THE FALL

Do you remember that Eve added to God's command by saying, "We are not to touch or eat from the tree of good and evil?" You can easily see that nothing good ever happens when God's Word is disobeyed, eschewed, or changed. When Eve took the forbidden fruit and held it in her hands, nothing in the physical realm seemed to be any different. Believing that to be true, she then ate of the fruit, and then, being fully deceived, she gave some to Adam, and he also ate.

Too late, like a bird caught in a snare, they both realized that what God had said was true. The protective covenant they enjoyed was removed, and as a result, their spirit person immediately died, but in mercy, God sent them out of the Garden to allow their bodies to finish the process of dying (asleep) as well. Had he allowed them to stay where the Tree of Life was present, they would have lived for all eternity with dead spirits and remained separated from their Creator. The only person of their three part being that was still alive was their soul, and whether in union with God or separated from God, the soul person will exist for all eternity somewhere.

BUT GOD ...

You will find that in all of your worst situations and trials, you can always look back or to the future and say, "but God." Adam and Eve could no longer enter into God's presence, so God, the good Shepherd, seeing that they were in trouble, went looking for them.

Meditate on this truth: The blood of a sacrificed animal could never remove the sins of man, but God, once again being rich in mercy, covered them with the skin of a slain animal, allowing that blood to be a temporary substitute covering for their sin. To completely remove their sin would require the blood of the last Adam, Jesus, who knew no sin.

There is a very definite purpose in taking time to revisit the remarkable story of beginnings, of the creation of Adam and Eve, and their original state before sin entered the picture. God wants you to have an unwavering knowledge and understanding that, as a born-again Christian, you are exactly like Adam and Eve before their fall. Without the full knowledge and understanding of what happened in the spirit realm, and in you at the moment of salvation, you will always struggle with your true identity in Christ.

Second Corinthians 5:17 says, *"Therefore, if anyone is*

in Christ, he is a new creation ..." (NKJV).

The Word of God (Truth) does not say that you are a restoration project with a few parts replaced and a new coat of paint applied in an attempt to hide the mars, scars, and scratches. It says that you are a New Creation!

FAST FORWARD

"For the grace of God has appeared, bringing salvation to all men" (Titus 2:11).

Grace and Jesus cannot be separated. They are both one and the same. Grace is the embodiment of Jesus and Jesus is the empowerment of grace. That is why Jesus said to the Apostle Paul, *"My grace is sufficient for you... "* (2 Corinthians 12:9). It was not, "Poor Paul, try to hang on and endure." It was exactly the opposite, more like a wakeup call of, "Paul, wake up and remember what you have been preaching." Christ is enough to both endure and overcome any adverse situation!

When Jesus, the only Son of God, came to earth preaching grace, everything, even time, fell under His rule and authority. Even today, time is referred to as being either B.C. or A.D. because time belongs to Him, and with Him, time is endless. For now, the Church is still enjoying the New Covenant of Grace, but very soon, that will change. At any time, at any moment, Christ could stand and call His Church unto Himself, bringing an end to the Church Age here on earth that we so richly enjoy.

Now, let's beat this drum once again because it has everything to do with your new ID! Without grace, no one who encountered death could ever be received into heaven because they were born of the corruptible seed of Adam.

The Law of Moses and the blood of animals were empowered to cover sin, but they were powerless to remove sin. That is not true of the powerful blood of Jesus, who was born of a virgin and fathered by the Holy Spirit. His blood completely eradicated sin and destroyed the sin nature that once held man captive (Romans 6:6). Because *"... grace has appeared, bringing salvation to all men"* (Titus 2:11), you are now a completely new person, born of the incorruptible seed of the last Adam, Jesus.

NICODEMUS AND YOU

Allow me to paraphrase to some degree an event recorded in the Gospel according to John 3:1-21. Rarely is a sermon preached or taught that includes all of these verses, but inside these treasured verses is one of the clearest of the many proclamations that Jesus made in identifying Himself as the Son of God, sent to earth to die for the sins of the world.

A man by the name of Nicodemus lived in Judah at the same time Jesus began His earthly ministry here on earth. He was a ruler of the Jews in the sense that he was a Pharisee, and he was also a member of the ruling Sanhedrin. The Sanhedrin Council was a group of men who made sure that the Law of Moses was carried out and obeyed by the Jews. Being in this group was a very prestigious position, and as with officials of our day, the position involved a lot of politics.

The Scriptures make it clear that Nicodemus was very aware of the miracle Man named Jesus. We don't know if he had seen some of the miracles himself, but we do know he knew of the miracles. Nicodemus wanted to know more about Jesus, so he chose to visit the home where He was staying, and he chose to visit him by night. Why did he choose to visit Jesus at night? That is a good question, and it's also a good time to pause and revisit the way you think.

Most Pharisees viewed Jesus as a heretic and an enemy of God. Because of this, being seen with Him could easily tarnish one's reputation. Therefore, it would seem logical to think and believe that Nicodemus went at night in order to protect his status and position. That may be a correct assumption, but then again, it may not be. A mind after the heart of God will conclude and be thankful that, for whatever reason, he was seeking to have an encounter with Jesus. It could be that he had responsibilities that kept him so busy that it forced him to visit the miracle Man at night, but in truth, we don't know why he chose to go there in the evening.

Why are we making such a point of why and when Nicodemus went to see Jesus? It's important because a carnal and judgmental mind will also be judgmental and condemning of loved ones and friends. A judgmental mindset will keep you bound by evil strongholds and in bondage to the Law. Judgmental mindsets will prevent you from being free and enjoying a great life and a great marriage. A little condemnation goes a long way.

Nicodemus began his conversation with Jesus by using truthful and flattering words. He said, "Rabbi, we know that you have come from God as a teacher, for no one can do these signs (miracles) that you do unless God is with him." Nicodemus was both generous and sincere when he addressed Jesus as Rabbi (teacher), and he was attempting to be both generous and genuine in saying that Jesus was able to do great miracles because God was with him. Nevertheless, he committed a major error in believing that Jesus' primary role was that of a teacher.

Jesus recognized his sincerity, but He also recognized the error, so He immediately cut to the chase and said, "Nicodemus, you must be born again." In essence, He was saying, "You are right, I was sent from God, but you need more than a Teacher; you need a Savior." Nicodemus was taken aback, and wanting to defend and justify himself, he dug his hole just a little bit deeper by replying, "... *How can a man be born when he is old? He cannot enter a second time into his mother's womb and be born, can he?*" (John 3:4).

The answer, of course, is, "No, we can't go back into our mother's womb," but Jesus was referring to the spiritual rebirth that every man and woman must experience before they can gain the proper ID for entrance into the Kingdom of God. Jesus explained that He was speaking in spiritual terms concerning the flesh and the spirit, but Nicodemus wasn't able to grasp what he was saying.

Jesus responded by gently and lovingly rebuking Nicodemus for not understanding because he should have known. Several prophets, including the one the Pharisees studied and quoted most often, the prophet Isaiah, had prophesied that God would send a Savior who would give a new heart and a new birth to the now dead spirit lying dormant in the heart of every living being. The book of Daniel even prophesied of the time that the Savior would appear, and the time of that prophecy's fulfillment had come.

"Jesus answered and said to him, 'Are you the teacher of Israel and do not understand these things?'" (John 3:10).

Again, a carnal mind will hear a harsh rebuke and

condemning words, but a mind set on Jesus will hear the voice of a loving and gentle Savior asking a life-changing question. Yes, Nicodemus should have known, but like so many people today, he had not searched the Scriptures for himself. His knowledge was based on what he perceived to be truth taught from others, not on the Truth found in the written Word of God. God's prophet Hosea (4:6) proclaimed, *"My people are destroyed for lack of knowledge,"* and they still are today.

Jesus continued to explain to Nicodemus that He is much more than a Rabbi. He is the only Son of God spoken of by Isaiah, and He is the Son of God sent to save a dying world. He told Nicodemus, *"For God so loved the world, that He gave His only begotten Son [Jesus], that whoever believes in Him shall not perish, but have eternal life"* (John 3:16).

What is eternal life? Eternal life is not that you will live forever because every person born of woman has a soul person who will live forever. The greater question is, "Where will your soul person spend eternity?" It will be either with God in heaven or in hell, separated from God. Take comfort from this: Hell wasn't created for you or any other person born of woman, Hell was created for Lucifer and his fallen angels. Ezekiel 18:32: *"'For I have no pleasure in the death of anyone who dies,' declares the Lord God. 'Therefore, repent and live'."* No man or woman will ever go to hell because it was predestined by God; instead they will spend eternity in hell because they refused to accept the redemptive work of Jesus on the Cross.

If eternal life is not us living forever, then what is it? The Apostle John records these words of Jesus: *"This is eternal life, that they may know You, the only true God, and Jesus*

Christ whom You have sent" (John 17:3). Was it possible for Nicodemus to be born again when he left the presence of Jesus? No, it wasn't possible at that exact moment in time. Jesus had yet to suffer the Cross and make the atonement for the sins of all mankind, but he could, like all Old Testament saints, be saved by putting his faith in God, for the Bible says of Abraham that "his faith was counted unto him as righteousness."

So what became of Nicodemus? He is seen a second time in Scripture boldly defending Jesus by confronting his fellow Pharisees who desired to send officers to arrest Him, with the intent of having Him stoned. He declared, *"... Our Law does not judge a man unless it first hears from him and knows what he is doing, does it?"* (John 7:50-51) He is seen a third time at the Cross of Jesus, after all of the Lord's disciples, save one, had fled. He came with a man named Joseph of Arimathea (John 19:39), and just to set the record straight, they both came during the day for all of Israel to see. They made a statement that transcended both status and position when they took the Lord's body down from an old rugged and bloodied Cross. *"... for he who is hanged is accursed of God ..."* (Deuteronomy 21:23).

Jesus took the curse (sin, sickness, poverty, and death) upon Himself when He went willingly to the Cross. He did not take just a part of the curse; He took all of the curse, and by His blood, He redeemed you completely from eternal death. The curse that once held you and all of mankind in captivity is now powerless. Satan can no longer control you through generational curses or any other demonic thing. Your sins have been atoned for—past, present, and future—and it gets even better. Not only have all of your sins been atoned for, but God promises that they will never be remembered again (Hebrews 8:12, Isaiah 43:25). While the curse remains in place for unbelievers, it no longer has any power or dominion over you because you have placed your faith in Jesus.

Perhaps you have read or heard 2 Corinthians 5:10 preached, *"For we must all appear before the judgment seat of Christ …"* It is true that every born-again believer will stand before the Judgment Seat of Christ *"so that each one may be recompensed for his deeds in the body, according to what he has done, whether good or bad."* We need to get a clear understanding of the purpose of the "Judgment Seat of Christ."

Hear this promise of the lord, *"And inasmuch as it is appointed for men to die once and after this comes judgment, so Christ also, having been offered once to bear the sins of many, will appear a second time for salvation without reference to sin, to those who eagerly await Him"* (Hebrews 9:27-28).

Only Christians will stand before the Judgment Seat of Christ, those whose names have been etched into the Lamb's Book of Life. You will not be there to be judged for your sins because Jesus Himself has already been judged for your sins and the sins of the whole world. You will stand before Him to give an account for every idle word spoken and every deed done with evil intentions or selfish motives. Idle words (words void of life) as well as good deeds that were done with the wrong motives will be judged for what they really were—wood, hay, and stubble. The large donation that everyone knew about will be burned up and counted as loss. Likewise, Jesus will give crowns for good deeds that were done with good and righteous motives.

Why is it important to receive crowns from Jesus? Because you will be given a special invitation to the Marriage Supper of the Lamb, and you will want to go there bearing gifts (crowns) to lay at the feet of Jesus. What a wonderful time that will be, but no child of God will want to show up empty handed and without gifts. The widow who placed her last cent into the Lord's treasury will be there; Mary and Martha will be there; Nicodemus and Joseph of Arimathea will be there; Moses and David will be there; and so will you. Every son and daughter will stand before the King of kings to receive their crowns, and you, dear soul, will receive yours as well. With crowns in hand, you will bow down and worship your precious Lord Jesus and place them at His feet.

That brings us to who our risen Christ says you are, to your real ID. You have already seen that what the Psalmist said is really true. You were fearfully and wonderfully made, a 3D person, being spirit, soul, and body. And now that you belong to Christ, your soul person has been saved and sealed by the work of the Holy Spirit. Your spirit person is now alive, born again of the incorruptible seed of God. You have a new nature, and you now have new DNA, the blood of Christ. Therefore, God says you are:

1. A New Creation—2 Corinthians 5:17
2. The Righteousness of God—2 Corinthians 5:21
3. Saint of God—Ephesians 1:1, Colossians 1:2
4. The Temple of the Holy Spirit—I Corinthians 3:16
5. An Ambassador for Christ—2 Corinthians 5:20
6. An Heir of God—Romans 8:17
7. A Child of God—John 1:12, John 3:2

This is a very short and abbreviated list of the many positive and wonderful names bestowed upon you when you were born again. Take careful notice that none of these refer to you as a sinner, or condemns you in any way. Not one writer of any of the epistles ever refers to God's Church as "old sinners saved by grace," so why would any born-again person say what God refuses to say? Before the Cross, Jesus spoke of Israel as being an evil and adulterous generation, but He also said that His Father would send the Holy Spirit to change its identification from evil and perverse to sanctified and righteous. That is the miracle of the Cross. It justified and reconciled you to the Father as though you had never sinned. Romans 8:1, *"Therefore there is now* [after what Jesus did] *no condemnation to those who are in Christ Jesus"* (bracketed words added for clarity). Jesus took your place on the Cross, and as an added bonus, He carried out and completed forever the Ministry of Death written in stone.

Listen to His final three words, *"It is finished!"* (John 19:30).

Do born-again believers still sin? Yes. When they allow their flesh to take the throne instead of the Holy Spirit, every Christian is very capable of sinning. That is why you must continually renew your mind to the Word of God. A renewed mind thinks on right living, not living in sin. A renewed mind is righteous conscious, not sin conscious. A born-again Christian has a new nature that wants to please God rather than displease Him.

The difference in your old identification and your new one could be compared to a hog and a sheep. Before you were saved, you had the nature of a hog, and wallowing in the mud and mire didn't bother you. Now that you are saved, you no longer have the nature of a hog. You have the new nature of a sheep, and sheep are never comfortable lying in the muck and mire. They want to be in green pastures. You can sin all you want to, but you no longer want to. The Holy Spirit is always reminding you of who you are, not who you were, and is continually leading you away from sin and to your High Priest Jesus. With your new ID in hand, Jesus is calling, *"... draw near with confidence to the throne room of grace ... receive mercy and find grace to help in time of need"* (Hebrews 4:16).

Your "old man" (nature) wanted to please the flesh; your "new man" (nature) wants to please Jesus. Your old heart loved the world but your new heart loves and yearns for Jesus. Your DNA is no longer the blood of Adam; it is now the DNA of Jesus. You now have a new ID because you are a New Creation in Christ Jesus, a citizen of the Kingdom of God. Therefore, let truth be truth and a lie a lie. You were an old sinner, but you have been saved by grace, and now you are who God says you are, the righteousness of God in Christ (2 Corinthians 5:21). You are a saint, a child of the King and blameless before Him. You are justified and sanctified by His Blood, not by works that any man should boast.

CAUTION!!! Carry your ID with you at all times. Like the old American Express commercials said, "Don't leave home without it!"

Chapter 3

You Have Kingdom Rights

Jesus said, *"But seek first His Kingdom and His righteousness, and all these things will be added to you"* (Matthew 6:33).

You may be wondering what all of this has to do with your pursuit of a great life and a great marriage, but rest assured that it has "everything" to do with possessing God's best for your life. If doing things the world's way hasn't worked out as planned, or facing the reality that there are still spiritual and physical voids in your life that need improvement, then let's continue on together and learn more of how to do things God's way.

You already know that your mind needs to be reprogrammed, and this is now a work in progress. You know who God says you are: a joint heir with Abraham through Christ Jesus. You know that God has set you free from sin and condemnation. You know that Jesus has a wonderful plan for your life, and you also know that Satan is powerless to keep you from obtaining it. You know your new ID has been signed and issued by Jesus Himself, and in Him and because of Him, His perfect love casts out all fear. Through growing confidence and overcoming faith, you are moving forward to take hold of God's best for both you and those you love.

You know that your new born-again ID gives you full access to Kingdom rights, but do you know what your Kingdom rights are? God wants you to know not only who you are in Him, but He wants you to know what your Kingdom rights are as well. When you understand your Kingdom rights, nothing can stand in the way of grabbing hold of everything God has for you.

Galatians 4:1 makes this declaration concerning born-again believers and the Kingdom, "… as long as the heir [you are the heir] is a child, he does not differ at all from a slave although he is owner of everything" (bracketed words added for clarity).

Paul compares the majority of Christian's lack of knowledge concerning their Kingdom rights to that of a child who is virtually clueless about an inheritance bequeathed to them by their wealthy parents. Therefore, there is very little distinction between God's covenant children, who have the vastness of the Kingdom of God at their disposal, and the unsaved, who must rely entirely on the world's system. It could be said with certainty that no one fully understands everything about their Kingdom rights because of its immeasurable riches, but the more revelation you gain, the more radical your life will change for the best. Even in God's Kingdom, there is a good, better, and best for you, so why not seek after God's best? When you finish your earthly life, you will live in perfect peace and victory with Jesus, but He wants you to rule and reign in the here and now, and this is where the rubber meets the road (Romans 5:17).

Why don't more Christians know and understand their Kingdom rights? Let's look again at this important truth because most Christians don't have the revelation that their new ID has given them access to everything God has. If you have been born again by the blood of Christ, you are already "of the Kingdom." One day, you will actually be "in the Kingdom," but you are now "of the Kingdom," possessing and having ownership of all of the riches it contains. Colossians 1:13-14 reveals this tremendous truth to everyone who has made Jesus their Champion and Lord, *"For He rescued us from the domain of darkness, and transferred us to the Kingdom of His beloved Son, in whom we have redemption, the forgiveness of sins."*

When Jesus preached to the large gathering of people on the mountainside, commonly known as "The Sermon on the Mount," He was reminding them that Israel was, is, and forevermore shall be His Covenant children. He taught on the Kingdom of God in order to redirect their hope for salvation away from the Laws of Moses, which were unable to clothe them in righteousness, couldn't feed them spiritually, and most importantly, couldn't save them, and point them to hope and faith in their Heavenly Father through a new and better covenant.

Almost five hundred years before Jesus came to earth, the prophet Zechariah said, "… *'Not by might, nor by power* [the Law], *but by My Spirit,' says the Lord of Hosts"* (bracketed words added for clarity). He then went on to tell how the Spirit would replace works when he declared, *"Grace, grace to it!"* (Zechariah 4:6-7). He was prophesying to Israel that a better covenant than the Law of Moses was on the horizon, and it would be a covenant of grace. God always keeps His Word, and His Word was fulfilled when He sent His Son Jesus, the essence of Grace, to earth in the form of a man.

Jesus, the Messiah, was preaching and instructing Israel to seek the Kingdom of God that is still to come. At that moment in time, it was beyond the comprehension of God's covenant people to understand that He would soon win a victory for them that would shatter the powers of hell, a victory that would allow them to be "of the Kingdom" here on earth. He won that victory, not only for Israel, but for the entire world, at the Cross of Calvary. Sad to say, countless numbers of saved Christians are still clueless that they are "of the Kingdom" in the here and now.

Once again, because it is so important that you understand and not be confused by errant doctrines, from a literary point of view, the Old Covenant ended with the Book of Malachi, and the New Covenant began with the first page of Matthew. From a doctrinal view, however, the Old Covenant ended at the Cross, and the New Covenant began when God the Father raised Jesus from the dead.

As a result of Christ's finished work on the Cross, you are no longer striving for victory because, spiritually speaking, you are already victorious. You are no longer seeking God's Kingdom because He has already transferred you to His Kingdom. Before the Cross, God allowed the blood of animals to be a substitute that could hide the sin of God's covenant people, but that blood was powerless to remove sin. That is why Jesus referred to Israel as an evil and adulterous generation (Matthew 7:11, Luke 11:13). The finished work of the Cross changed the relationship between God and man forever because the Cross completely removed all evidence of sin. The psalmist declared of a coming day, *"This is the day which the Lord has made; let us rejoice and be glad in it"* (Psalm 118:24). He wasn't speaking of the current day, but of a future day, the day of the Cross. The Holy Scripture, the voice of God, now stands at the blood-soaked Cross of Calvary and calls out to everyone with eyes that see and ears that hear, that Jesus has robed all of His children in His "Righteousness" (2 Corinthians 5:21). Jesus is now our High Priest and advocate and has issued a standing invitation for you to enter with confidence into the throne room of grace and mercy. His invitation is always open because you are His own, made spiritually clean and spiritually righteous by His blood.

DID YOU KNOW???

Did you know that before the Cross, Satan was the accuser of the brethren? He accused a man by the name of Job; not only him, but all of God's Covenant people. They did not have all of the Kingdom rights that you so richly enjoy today, but God, who is rich in mercy, watched over and provided for them and protected them from destruction because He had established a Covenant with Israel. Under the New Covenant, Satan can no longer accuse you before God because Jesus Christ is also your attorney and legal counselor who stands eternally in the way of your accuser, declaring you "Not guilty!" to His Father.

In the spirit realm, you are now an identical picture of the Prodigal son who left sin behind and went to his Father's house. The father said of the son who came home, *"... this brother of yours was dead and has begun to live, and was lost and has been found"* (Luke 15:32). You were like that son, but now that you have come home, you are also robed in righteousness, and the Blood of Jesus is over your door, making you perfect in the Father's eyes. You now have a ring on your finger signifying that you are the bride of Christ, having absolute authority over your enemy and granting you full access to all of God's goodness and promises.

God commanded Moses and Joshua to take off their shoes when they came into His presence because they stood on Holy Ground. That was the Old Covenant. Under the New Covenant it was just the opposite. When the Prodigal son came home and stepped onto "holy ground," his father commanded sandals to be placed on his feet, thereby sending a forceful message to the kingdom of darkness that he was an heir of God through His Son Jesus. You are an heir also, dressed and adorned exactly as the Prodigal was dressed, and for you also, a fatted calf has been given. The fatted calf represents the extravagance of God's love and gifts that Jesus purchased for you when He went to the Cross. God is not withholding any good thing.

Seem too good to be true? It's not. It's all true! That is who you are, and no power of hell, no, nothing short of unbelief can deprive you of your Kingdom rights.

"Do not be deceived, my beloved brethren. Every good thing given and every perfect gift is from above, coming down from the Father of lights, with whom there is no variation, or shifting shadow" (James 1:16-17).

Perhaps you have heard that "God is good, but for your own good, He will use sickness, accidents, and financial ruin to get your attention and teach you something." The reason, we are told, is to draw you closer to Him. Scripture does not validate such theology. That type of teaching is error, and no matter how well-meaning it may be, this doesn't change the truth that the Cross ended the enmity between God's elect and Himself. It is, in reality, an untruth that the enemy uses to hinder the relationship between believers and their heavenly Father. You have to disregard the Scriptures and the Cross to believe this type of errant teaching. God's judgment for sin was placed entirely on Jesus at the Cross. Not some of it, but all of it. Enmity and war has been replaced with peace between God and those who trust in His Son for salvation. The curse for the unsaved and unrepentant world is still in place, but not for you if you have been born again. For you, the curse is broken and no longer has any power over your life.

What does the Scripture say? It bears repeating, *"Every good thing given and every perfect gift is from above, coming down from the Father of lights, with whom there is no variation, or shifting shadow"* (James 1:17).

God then declares to anyone with ears to hear and eyes to see that this Scripture and representation of Him is an absolute. In other words, He doesn't send good gifts one day and bad gifts the next. He is not a shifting shadow. No, He is the same yesterday, today, and forever. God has not changed and is unchanging, but the covenant between Him and man did change. How? An exchange was made. The old was exchanged for the new, from a covenant of Law and Judgment to a covenant of Grace and Liberty. (Read Hebrews 8:6.)

God is Love, and God is Holy, and because He is holy, your sin debt had to be paid in full before you could enter into the throne room of grace. Therefore, Jesus paid your debt, all of it, in full on the Cross. Because He is love, you are no longer under Law or judgment; you are under the New Covenant of Grace and the Law of Liberty. God never mixes the two covenants, but that is not true of many well-meaning pastors and teachers who generously mix law and grace in their messages. The result of this type of errant teaching is that many of God's children see themselves as condemned, confused, and discouraged with life. Sunday after Sunday, day after day, they feel they must rededicate their lives to Jesus and try once more to please Him by their own efforts and works. No wonder the Church, *per se*, doesn't believe in miracles, nor does it expect to see the power of God displayed. Condemnation births unbelief, and unbelief corrupts true faith, but you, dearly beloved, are no longer under condemnation, but grace.

IS GOD SOVEREIGN???

Is God sovereign? The answer, of course, is, "Yes, God is Sovereign!" If God isn't sovereign, then Christianity is a hoax, and we have all been duped. But He is sovereign, and you have done well by placing your faith in Him. No one but a sovereign God could speak through the prophets and then ensure their prophecies would come to pass exactly as He said. Only a sovereign God could prophesy of a Savior that would come to earth to be born of a virgin, when He would be born, where He would be born, the exact lineage he would come from, how He would die, where He would be buried, and that He would rise on the third day. God did all of that and much more. Yes, God is sovereign!

Does the fact that God is sovereign mean that absolutely nothing happens on earth unless it's His will? The answer is, "No!" It may be convenient to put the responsibility of everything that happens in life on God, but this doesn't make it true. God is sovereign, but He delegated the authority to rule over the earth to Adam, who then allowed Satan to steal it. The idea that we are all pawns in God's hands and nothing happens unless He decrees it is not scriptural. God's will was made perfectly clear to Adam that he was not to eat from the Tree of the Knowledge of Good and Evil, but Adam did so anyway. Adam was given the freedom of choice, to obey or disobey, and he chose to disobey. It becomes quite obvious that God's will is not always done here on earth, but this does not mean that God is not sovereign.

To say that all of the terrible things taking place every minute of every day around the world were orchestrated by God, or was God's will, or even His permissive will, is an egregious doctrinal error. God is not giving a tacit nod to child abuse, rape, murder, oppression, disease, and world hunger. He is not causing children to die young from sickness, disease, drugs, and alcohol. He is not the one who causes a bad wreck or sickness to take the life of a teenager or young parent. No, God is not the cause, no matter how convenient it may be to say that He is. We live in a fallen world, and accidents happen. People sometimes make bad choices, and bad things happen because of them, but that is not God's fault. It isn't God's fault that the world is continually at war and people are dying and children are starving. In fact, Jesus told the Church to feed the hungry and minster to the sick. He is not causing chaos and death just so the Church will have something to do. One day Jesus will return and put a stop to all of the bad and evil that now surrounds us, but until then the Church is His hands and feet, His mouth and His ambassador, empowered to carry out His will.

With great simplicity, God spoke through His prophet Jeremiah and declared, *"... I am watching over My word to preform it"* (Jeremiah 1:12). Today, it is obvious that an ever-increasing number of pastors and teachers are receiving more and more revelation of the grace and power that belong to the Church. The result is that more and more people are being healed and filled with the Holy Spirit. God is the Guarantor of every promise that belongs to His Kingdom, and there is no shortage of His promises. How does it work? Let's look together.

THE TONGUE

Receiving and understanding revelation truth concerning the tongue and the power of your words is absolutely essential in learning to live your life in the victorious dominion of God's Kingdom, so let's get started.

Have you ever heard the children's rhyme: "Sticks and stones may break my bones, but words will never hurt me"? Sounds like a children's nah-nah, and it is. But it isn't just a children's nah-nah, it is a terrible lie. Words do have the power to hurt and destroy. Just check out the divorce rate. Secondly, children whose parents use or allow them to use words to hurt others tend to grow up and do the same. Your words are powerful seeds that will germinate and shape your future. Remember, in the beginning, God created the entire universe and everything that is seen and not seen by the power of His spoken words. Remember also that Jesus defeated Satan by speaking the written Word to him, and so will you.

ADD WISDOM

Proverbs is a great Book of knowledge and wisdom. I highly encourage men and women, but especially men, to read from it on a daily basis, remembering always that it must be read in light of the New Covenant. The Old Covenant is "Do." The New Covenant is "Done."

Proverbs contains thirty-one chapters that correspond to the months containing the most days, so a simple way to keep moving forward is to read and study the chapter that corresponds to the current day. Remember, God is not going to be upset if you miss a day, but making it a part of your daily devotion time will give you immeasurable wisdom to excel in business, marriage, and relationships. Now, let's retrieve one of God's pearls of wisdom from Proverbs 18 and begin applying it to your life.

"With the fruit of a man's mouth his stomach will be satisfied; He will be satisfied with the product of his lips. Death and life are in the power of the tongue" (Proverbs 18:20-21).

The reason so many lives are in disarray, marriages destroyed, bodies sick, and finances in ruin can usually be traced back to the way a person thinks, their knowledge of God's Word, and the words they have spoken into existence. Your words will either produce life or they will produce death. There is no gray area. They will always produce the fruit that comes from your mouth, and depending on the words you speak (seeds), you will end up eating good fruit or bad fruit. This truth is easy to confirm. If you listen closely to what people are saying, you will quickly see and discern that their words reflect their current lives. People who continually speak about their illnesses or financial woes as if they are their only plight in life will always battle with discouragement, sickness, and lack.

Jesus said, *"The thief comes only to steal and kill and destroy; I came that they may have life, and have it abundantly"* (John 10:10). The last phrase of this verse can also be translated *"have abundance."* It would then read: *"... I came that they may have life, and have abundance."*

Do you see the mission and objective of each one in this verse? The thief has one goal in mind, to steal your dreams, rob you of good health, and destroy your marriage and your future. How can he accomplish that? He accomplishes it by stealing the spoken word. When I was a young man, I found that the enemy was very adept at stealing God's Word before it became rooted in my heart and mind, so I prayed for victory to overcome the thief. The Holy Spirit began prompting me to write down His thoughts and plans when I received them, and not just write them down, but to study and meditate on them as well. He also showed me that I must search His Word for myself and that it was up to me to speak His promises and blessing into my life and the lives of my loved ones. In time, His words moved from the pages of my notes and became firmly planted in my heart and mind. Let's be in agreement that the same will be true for you because God is no respecter of persons.

Let me now inject another word of caution, and then accentuate it with the Lord's plan to give you an abundant life. Never call things that are as though they are not. Rather, the command is to call things that are not as though they are (Romans 4:17). Is there a difference? Yes, there is a one hundred and eighty degree difference. It works like this. If you were to receive a bad report concerning anything in your body, finances, etc., it would be stupid to say that the report is not a fact and state that those things don't exist because the truth is that they do exist. However, you become fodder for the enemy when you come into agreement with a bad report. God's promises are always able to triumph over facts. The bad report may be factual, but God says that you are a joint heir with Him, and your quest for a great life and great marriage are the desires of His heart. God always watches over His Word to perform it, and that is truth.

FACTS vs. TRUTH

Several years ago my wife was diagnosed with fibromyalgia, a very debilitating disease that is both painful and life threatening. At that time, I had not been taught that life and death are in the power of the tongue. Neither had I ever heard it preached or taught that "God wants you well." Because of this, I wrestled with the teaching that God would at times cause sickness to get our attention or to punish us for His own reasons. Listen closely, I am not questioning a preacher's or teacher's love for God if they don't believe that miracles and healings are for today, but I do believe that they need more revelation concerning healing and miracles. Far too many pastors and teachers embrace what they have been taught instead of searching the Scriptures for themselves.

The facts given to me were this: Your wife has a degenerative disease that is incurable. One doctor and close friend confided to me in private, "Her good days will be bad days, but she will just have to learn to live with it." At the time, I didn't have the answer, but my spirit person told me not to accept the facts as presented by the experts, so as never before, I began crying out to the Lord in prayer and supplication. My wife, who had always been a very beautiful, fun, and outgoing person was, at that time, anything but fun and outgoing. She was in constant pain, unable to function, and with each passing day, she was becoming more and more captive to her bed. BUT GOD, who is the Author and Finisher of our faith, stepped in, and through His sovereign prompting, He caused me to sit down in front of a television early one morning.

Watching morning TV was not normal for me. My morning routine consisted of enjoying a cup of coffee, reading the Word of God, and praying and seeking for fresh wisdom and direction from the Holy Spirit. As I sat in front of the TV, a heavy spirit of defeat began closing in on me. I had prayed for my wife's healing since the inception of her sickness, but it seemed that God had turned a deaf ear to me. As I surfed through the different channels, I saw a man sitting in a chair, teaching the Word of God. I was preparing to go to another channel when the words, "God wants you well," flashed across the screen. Those words got my attention! For the next three weeks, and without my wife's knowledge, I sat in front of the TV, coffee in hand, and began receiving a much-needed transformation of my mind concerning God's willingness to heal.

He began explaining that God's children have Kingdom rights, and one of those very important rights includes His desire for us to walk in divine health. He gave Scriptures that seemed to jump right off the pages of God's Word, finding their mark in my heart, soul, and mind. Scriptures like: "... *by His stripes we are healed*" (Isaiah 53:5 NKJV).

"... Who heals all of your diseases" (Psalm103:3). *"Beloved, I pray that in all respects you may prosper and be in good health, just as your soul prospers"* (3 John 2). Wow! Faith began to arise, but the icing on the cake came when he explained a couple of life-changing verses found in Mark 11:23-24.

"WHOEVER SAYS unto the mountain, 'Be taken up and cast into the sea,' and does not doubt in his heart, but BELIEVES that what he SAYS is going to happen, it will be granted him. Therefore I say to you, all things for which you pray and ask, BELIEVE that you have received them, and they will be granted you" (emphasis added).

Our mountain at the time was fibromyalgia, but yours is probably different. You may be facing many mountains, but that doesn't matter to God because no mountain is too big, no challenge is so great that it can stand against God's spoken word when faith is included. I had prayed, begged, and pleaded with God to heal my wife for over two months, but she had become increasingly worse. I found myself becoming angry with God. (Have you ever been mad at God?) But it wasn't God's fault, and because He knew my heart, His mercy and grace continued to pursue me. He had given me the truth in His Word, but, like Nicodemus, I had not searched the Scriptures for myself. Now, armed with His Word and knowing that it was His will to heal and that the provision for healing has already been made, I prayed a prayer that was saturated with faith over my wife. I spoke to the fibromyalgia in the name of Jesus and commanded it to leave her body. My beautiful wife was healed, made whole, and now, more than a decade later, she continues to remain healed and whole.

You, dear reader, have been given the same delegated authority to speak to any mountain that is hindering you from receiving God's best. So begin speaking life!

If your mountain is finances, start tithing and speak God's word to it; speak words such as, *"My God supplies all of my needs according to His riches in Glory in Christ Jesus"* (Philippians 4:19). *"The young lions do lack and suffer hunger; but they who seek the LORD shall not be in want of any good thing"* (Psalm 34:10).

If it's sickness, then declare promises such as, *"He was crushed for my well-being; the chastening for my well-being fell upon Him, and by His Stripes I am healed"* (Isaiah 53:5). That, by the way, is present tense. Healing is not something He may do or may not do; it's part of the atonement paid for in full at the Cross. Jesus has already provided for your healing!

If it's a broken relationship, divorce, or children who seem to be going the way of the world, speak to it and say, *"'For I know the plans that I have for you,' declares the Lord, 'plans for welfare and not for calamity ... '"* (Jeremiah 29:11). (Insert appropriate names.) *"... bearing with one another, and forgiving each other: even as Christ forgave me, so I also will do"* (Colossians 3:13).

If divorce has already occurred or your business has gone under, speak God's Word and say, *"My God causes all things to work together for good to me because I love God, and I have been called according to His will and purpose"* (Romans 8:28).

If it's a stronghold or strongholds, then stop speaking and agreeing with the enemy that he has a stronghold in your life. Instead, begin to declare, *"The Lord is my salvation, the stronghold of my life"* (Psalm 27:1).

In every crisis or negative situation that arises, you can always declare, *"No weapon formed against you (me) can prosper"* (Isaiah 54:17).

Do you get the picture? You are not a defenseless, defeated person without hope, living on a dead end street. You are who God says you are, His champion who can overcome every situation with the sword of His Word spoken in faith. Notice that some of these verses have purposely been changed into a personal tense, but God doesn't mind, in fact, He wants you to make them your own. Always end each Scripture and prayer with "In Jesus' name, Amen" because the power is in the Sovereign Name of Jesus spoken in faith.

As you learn to guard your words and begin using your God-given delegated authority, your life and circumstances will begin to change. If you don't see things change as quickly as you might hope, remember that the Kingdom is all about seed time and harvest. Jesus said it this way, *"... first the blade, then the ear, after that the full corn in the ear"* (Mark 4:28 KJV). In other words, you must allow God's Word to have time to work. Don't set a time frame or try to instruct God on how to take care of your needs because His ways are not our ways. But He will do it, and it is impossible for His Word to fail. Some obstacles will move quickly, while others may take more time. In everything remain steadfast and patient, and in everything, "Trust in the LORD with all your heart and do not lean on your own understanding" (Proverbs 3:5).

Chapter 4

Expect Good Things
(Because Christ Loves You)

As you continue to grow in your knowledge of God and begin seeing Him as He really is, it will become progressively easier to expect good things to happen in your life. In the same way that you desire good things for your children, your heavenly Father has an enormously greater desire to do good things for you. His river of grace and mercy are effortlessly and endlessly overflowing into your life with an open invitation to drink and not be thirsty. You can go to the river and drink from a cup, a glass, or better still, you can jump in and be completely saturated. Receiving from Him always depends on how you see Him, and just as importantly, how you think He sees you.

God's river of abundance isn't based on either your faithfulness or unfaithfulness. Instead, it is based entirely on Jesus' faithfulness to carry out the wishes of His Father, even to the Cross. It's based on the reality that you are a covenant child of God and that God takes care of His children. It flows with living water because God wants you to prosper and walk in divine health. The abundance flows to enable you to sow into His Kingdom and into ministries that are preaching the "Good News Gospel" to a lost and dying world. It flows because God takes great pleasure in seeing you enjoy a great life and a great marriage. He never stops the flow because you are at times unfaithful, although it may seem that way when sin or bad judgment opens a door and allows the enemy to operate in your life.

As you continue the process of renewing your mind with the Word of God, your needs will always be taken care of, your personal relationships will begin to flourish, and the peace of God will begin to settle in and take control of your mind and emotions. This doesn't mean that there will never be testing and trials in your life, but it does mean that they will no longer be able to seduce and triumph over you as they once did. Instead, they will become stepping stones and faith builders for your future.

CHRIST, OUR FIRST LOVE

May I ask you a question? Would you be willing to take a few moments and walk with me down a wonderful path that is absolutely life changing? I have been on this walk for many, many years, and it never grows old or becomes wearisome. I believe it will be the same for you. We have never met, but through Christ Jesus, I really do know you. Even though I don't know what you are going through, I do know what you are going though. People traveling through this life get wounded, pierced, and hurt. People are people no matter their status or position in life. No one is exempt; everyone goes through things, but going through it is much easier when you have friends who will stand with you in love, even during the times when you are unlovable. We all need personal relationships like that, but it may be that you don't currently have any friends who are willing to stand with you, and you feel alone. Take heart and be encouraged because Jesus has promised to never leave nor forsake you, and He always keeps His promises. It is in Him, and through Him, that you are now becoming completely free of past failures, hurts, and fears. You are becoming the conqueror God intended you to be, and your future is looking much, much, brighter.

As you begin this walk and begin spending time with Jesus, you will find that those moments will prove to be the most wonderful satisfying moments of your entire life. People have often asked me how much time I spend alone with God, both through meditating on His Word and in prayer, and my answer is simply, "Not enough." I am considered an early morning person, and from the time I was a young man in my late twenties until the present, spending time alone with Him in the early mornings is a time I relish. This schedule has worked out great for my family and me.

You may not be an early morning person; you may be the exact opposite. Regardless of which kind of person you are, let me encourage you to begin spending time alone with the Lord. It's not about the amount of time you spend seeking Him and His Kingdom because God is not wearing a stopwatch or keeping score. It's simply about spending time alone with Him. You may be an alone mom who gets up early and works late trying to make ends meet, and your body is simply too tired to stop and have your own time alone with Christ. That's okay. He understands, but what you can do is learn to speak to Him as you lie in bed or spend time in prayer and praise while traveling in your car. As you begin spending time with Him, He will begin sending supernatural wisdom and needed answers into your heart. As Jesus becomes your first love, life itself will become far more enjoyable and much easier to manage. His plan is a far more excellent plan than any you could ever conceive of, so allow Him to have His way. The excellence of your future is yours for the taking, and you can receive it by being willing to place your hope in the finished work of Jesus. What is the finished work of Jesus? It is Shalom, nothing broken and nothing missing.

Caution! Don't neglect spending quality time with your loved ones as well. Countless pastors, evangelists, teachers, and even common laypeople have made the mistake of putting ministry ahead of family, and this is totally different than spending quality time with the Lord. Law in any form will have a tendency to lead to a type of rigid, judgmental religion.

HOPE

A particular picture has hung on my office wall for more than thirty years and is now one of my most treasured keepsakes. It is a painting of a small river that becomes increasingly smaller until it finally appears to trickle to a dead end, but when your eyes look past the small trickle of water, you discover that rather than ending, it is actually connected to a large beautiful lake. It reads, "What seems to be the end may really be a new beginning." There were days when I avoided looking at the picture because the trickle of water seemed to be where I was living my life. Then there were other days when God would direct my eyes to the lake, not allowing me to forget that Christ lives in me, and that He and He alone is the Hope of glory

(Colossians 1:27).

In this same way, Christ wants you to know that your life is headed toward a new beginning, one full of His majesty, love, and abundance. You are His pet, His star student, the apple of His eye. Believe it because it's true! Your picture is the big one on the center of His refrigerator, and when you look at it carefully with spiritual eyes, you will see that there is a spot on your forehead. Unlike the red dot (bindi) worn for decoration by women of Eastern religions, this spot is the stigmata of the shed blood of Jesus, the Passover Lamb.

God loves you unconditionally and is very jealous over all of His children. He has commanded all of heaven's resources to be made available to you whenever you ask for anything in the name of His Son Jesus. He has ordered His mighty angels to minister to your needs and protect you when you lie down and when you rise up, when you go out and when you come in. He is guarding over you 24/7, and in the midst of all of this He is causing the impossible to become possible. As you pray and spend time with Him (He isn't keeping score), He will continually send forth His angels to ensure your needs are met, and it will be done with overflowing abundance.

"Are they not all ministering spirits [speaking of angels] *sent out to render service for the sake of those who will inherit salvation?"* (Hebrews 1:14 bracketed words added for clarity).

"Bless the Lord, you His angels, mighty in strength, who perform His word, obeying the voice of His word!" (Psalm 103:20).

It is easy to see that placing your hope in Christ and His reigning Kingdom is a good place to be because He watches over His word to perform it. You can now get up each morning and give praise to Him for a good night's sleep, a warm bed, shelter over your head, and for food to eat. You can praise Him for guiding you through each moment of every day because it is a day He wants you to live and enjoy, trusting in Him completely. It's hard for the finite mind to fathom, but God has already lived today and tomorrow, and He has already walked wherever it is you are going to walk. That is why the Word says, *"Your word is a lamp to my feet and a light to my path"* (Psalm 119:105).

His favor is over you in little things as well as things that appear to be bigger than life. He will give you the parking place you need (when you really need it), as well as the home you desire. He will heal your body, your emotions, and your finances. He will lead wonderfully Spirit-filled Christians into your life and allow them to bless you as you return the blessings to His Kingdom. You will be reminded of the miracles recorded in the Bible and come to realize that miracles are for today. There will no longer be more month than money as you listen to the voice of the Holy Spirit and become wiser and more discerning with your spending habits. Sickness and disease will have to pack up and leave because every curse, even generational curses, have been broken. Yes, all of these things and more are God's desire for your well being. God wants you to place all of your hope in Him and be made whole. Will you do it? Never forget that hope is an amazing, uncompromising phenomenon when it's rooted in Jesus, but the Lord will not allow you to rest in hope alone. His desire is to show you that hope will become fully manifested when it becomes rooted in faith.

FAITH

"Now faith is the assurance of things hoped for, the conviction of things not seen" (Hebrews 11:1).

Notice that the word "hope" has "ed" attached to the end of it, thus denoting a past tense. You began with hope, but the "ed" says that it has now turned into faith. You are still unable to see what you were hoping for, but because you are aligned with God's Word and His promises, you now have total faith that what you hoped for is now going to come to pass. Faith does not rest in what it can see, rather it takes hold of things not yet seen as being a provision that is going to come to pass. The timing and the way it happens are now in the hands of the Lord.

Concerning your faith, let's take a close look at what faith is and what it is not. On numerous occasions, and most especially when talking to His disciples, Jesus used the term "little faith," while at other times He used the term "great faith." What do those two terms mean? What do they mean to you? These are very important questions because faith is the key that unlocks all of God's promises.

Let's begin with this: Little faith and great faith are not descriptive of size. Jesus used each of these terms to characterize a person's ability to either believe or not believe. Most Christians only see those terms relative to the size of their faith, but that is not what Jesus meant. Size by itself does not determine power. For instance, even though an atom cannot be seen with the naked eye, we know it exists. We also know that despite its miniscule size, there is tremendous power inside a harnessed atom, enough to destroy a city. The Son of God said, *"... if you have faith the size of a mustard seed, you will say to this mountain, 'Move from here to there,' and it will move; and nothing will be impossible to you"* (Matthew 17:20). Jesus purposely used this seed to illustrate His point because a mustard seed is one of the smallest seeds that can be seen with the naked eye. We know from His own words that little faith is not relative to size. Rather, it represents one's ability to believe that prayers or spoken words that align with Kingdom promises must come to pass.

When Jesus spoke to His disciples about their little faith, He was always referring to a faith that did not work. He used the term "little faith" when they were unable to cast a demon out of the young boy whose father brought him to them (Matthew 17:19-20), and again when a great storm arose as they were crossing the Sea of Galilee (Matthew 8:26). Every time He spoke concerning someone's "great faith," such as the centurion we read about in Matthew 8:8-13, it was a faith that worked. Little faith must see before it will believe, while great faith believes it will happen before it is ever seen. Little faith is unbelief; great faith is believing. Little faith never works because it is rooted in the natural, while great faith always works because it is rooted in the supernatural rather than the physical.

How can you grow your faith? God tells us in Romans 10:17, *"So faith comes from hearing, and hearing by the word of Christ."* It will not come any other way. Your faith must be rooted in the Word of God. If it's rooted in anything else, unbelief will triumph, and failure is sure to follow. God wants you to trust Him and Him alone, but He is full of grace and mercy and always willing to meet you wherever your point of faith is. If your faith for healing is currently rooted in doctors and medicine, He will meet you there and use them to get you healed. If your faith is currently rooted in the world's financial system of banks and borrowing, He will meet you there and allow them to help meet your financial needs.

The challenge with both is that these are only band-aid fixes, and the same challenges will continue to reoccur over and over again. Know this with certainty, God doesn't want you sick, and He doesn't want you in debt. Don't become frustrated if that is where you currently find yourself, but determine in your heart not to stay in the world's system. God's system works much better, and it's without cost because Jesus has already paid for all of your needs in full. He won't send you a large medical bill at the end of the month, and He doesn't charge interest on the countless provisions He sends your way. In fact, He will send you interest you didn't earn of thirty, sixty, and even a hundred fold. Expect God to meet your needs! Expect Him to give you a miracle! Expect the righteous (you!) to be healed and to prosper because that is God's will for your life!

Now, dear reader, concerning hope and faith, do not think that hope is any less than faith because hope validates faith and faith validates hope. Paul wrote, *"Now may the God of hope fill you with all joy and peace in believing, so that you will abound in hope by the power of the Holy Spirit"* (Romans 15:13). It may be that you are almost without hope in your marriage, and the love that was once there is now missing. You may be struggling in your finances, and it seems that you are sinking ever deeper into debt. It may be that your children have gone the way of the world, and have closed their ears and hearts to your countless efforts to reach them. It may be that you are staring divorce in the face, or that divorce has already taken its toll on your life. All of these things are troubling and painful to your soul. But, dear one, God has not forsaken you, and He will deliver you from every scheme of the enemy. He will place you back on solid ground when you place your hope and faith in Him. Look once again into the lovely face of Jesus and allow Him to love you and reach deep into your heart so that the healing process can begin. Jesus, the great Physician, the greatest of all heart surgeons, will heal and restore your life. He not only can do it, He wants to do it. Let Him.

LOVE

From Genesis to Revelation, from the first Book to the last Book, you will discover a thin, but strong, Red Thread that binds all of the individual Books together into one. That thread is strong and unbreakable because it is actually the blood of Jesus. When Adam and Eve got into trouble, God went looking for them, and the Good Shepherd had one thing in mind, to save them and bring them back into relationship with Him. You may think that you were looking for Him first, but the truth is He came looking for you long before your decision to say "Yes" to Him. Why did He do it? It's called LOVE!

John, the apostle who lived and walked with Jesus during His three and a half year ministry here on earth, wrote, *"... God is love"* (1 John 4:8)! Love is the very essence, the personification of who God is. As you look at and examine the ministry of Jesus, you will find that He never refused healing to anyone. He forgave the sins of an adulteress, a lying friend, and a thief. He provided food for five thousand men and, again, for another four thousand, not to mention the additional thousands of women and children who were with them. John wrote that there are not enough books to contain the many miracles performed by Jesus (John 21:25).

It was unconditional love that empowered Jesus to stand before Pilate and remain silent, knowing that to do so would seal the inevitable verdict of "Guilty." Consider the unending love of Jesus when He willingly fulfilled the prophecy of Isaiah 53 and took the terrible and horrific lashing of a Roman whip on His body so that your body could be healed. That horrific beating would have killed many men, but the Father's love for you said His life could not end at the end of a whip, or a sword, or by stoning; it had to end on the Cross, one of the most horrific forms of death imaginable. Consider carefully the prophecy of David in Psalm 22 as he looked into the future and saw Jesus hanging on a tree in naked shame, suffering as no man had ever suffered.

Jesus and His disciples were well acquainted with Roman crucifixion, the cross of death. Crosses were commonly used by the Romans during the days when Jesus ministered. Undoubtedly, He and His disciples saw many men hanging in agony or already dead on crude, makeshift crosses as they traveled about from city to city. It's no wonder that Jesus agonized and asked of His Father, *"Father, if You are willing, remove this cup from Me; yet not My will, but Yours be done"* (Luke 22:42).

Jesus was not asking this because He didn't know the will of the Father. He was asking because He did know the will of the Father. He was all God, but He was also all human, and His flesh rebelled at the horrific thought of dying on a Roman cross. Today, Christians will sometimes pray, "Thy will be done," meaning, *Que sera, sera,* or "what ever will be will be," but this philosophy is an error. Jesus knew the will of God, and so can every Christian. His will is revealed in the Holy Bible, His last will and testament. It can be found from Genesis to Revelation within the inerrant, infallible, Word of God.

What made His suffering greater than even the agony of the cross was the cup of sin that He willingly drank that contained every vile sickness and disease ever known or committed by man. These same sicknesses were empowered to manifest themselves in and on His body as He hung on the Cross. It's no wonder that the Scriptures declare, *"His visage was marred more than any man, and His form more than the sons of men"* (Isaiah 52:14 NKJV). Consider that Jesus bore the curse and died for all mankind, yet his love is an individual love so that if there had been no one but you, He would have suffered and died for you alone. The Cross, and the Cross alone, is the epitome, the highest apex, by which all other love must be measured. God is Love.

With that type of love, all other love seems to fade and shrink into the shadows, but God, who loved you to the Cross, has made only one simple but life-changing request of you, and that is to love Him more than the things of the world, to love Him as He loves the Church. Jesus said, here is my commandment, *"And you shall love the LORD your God with all your heart, with all of your soul, and with all of your mind, and with all of your strength …"* (Mark 12:30).

When you love God above everything and everyone else, you can then go on to love others, even the unlovely.

You can love those who have deeply wounded you because the power of grace will enable you to do exactly that. Jesus wants you to forgive because unforgiveness is a huge weapon that the enemy will use to attack and penetrate your mind, heart, and soul. Unforgiveness has the power to stain and corrupt not only you, but others as well, even those you love and don't want to hurt. If that were not enough, an unforgiving sprit will always be a major stumbling block that will hinder your relationship with Jesus. Jesus wants you to return good for evil, love for malice, kindness for contempt, and respond to harsh words with gentle words.

The often heard and used statement, "I can't forgive them for what they did to me" are words the enemy loves to hear. He knows that a heart filled with unforgiveness represents an open door that allows him free access to steal, kill, and destroy. Unforgiveness will make the heart and soul sick, and very often it will result in a sick and diseased body as well. The flip side of this is that praying a blessing over someone who has wounded you will allow God to change your heart toward that person. Be honest with God and tell Him what He already knows, that you are praying out of obedience (Matthew 5:44) to His Word, but you are having trouble being sincere. In time, a heart change will begin to manifest itself, and all of the hurt and resentment will be washed away. It is then that freedom will come, and you will have the liberty to pray in love and ask God's richest blessings on their life. Only God can change a heart and replace hate with love. It bears repeating that you can't change yourself; only God can do that, but let's give praises to Him, for He is washing and cleansing your heart even at this very moment.

Consider now the gifts of Faith, Hope, and Love that the Father has so richly and freely given to you. What will you do with them? For starters, you can begin to expect good things to fill and saturate your life. You can begin by casting down every vain thought and imagination that tries to exalt itself above these three great gifts; by doing so you can then take hold of the things that are good and lovely. You can take control of your thought life and begin speaking positive, faith-filled words. The result will be that good things will overcome the negative, replacing it with happiness, joy, and fulfillment. God will do it!

Chapter 5

Words Are Powerful

"Behold, the sower went out to sow." (Mark 4:3)
"The sower sows the word." (Mark 4:14)

A seed is one of the most interesting and invaluable species of all God's creation. In brief, it is actually a fertilized embryo encased in a covering called the testa, complete with its own food supply. Amazingly, science has discovered that seeds can live in a state of dormancy for hundreds, even thousands, of years as long as they are safe from moisture. You may have held various types of seeds in your hands before, and in all probability you have planted a few and seen that there is indeed life in them. That is why Jesus chose to use a seed to illustrate the power of words.

Proverbs 18:21 says; *"Death and life are in the power of the tongue …"* While life is in the seed, it will remain unproductive until it is placed into soil and watered. In the same way, your thoughts are unproductive until they become words spoken in faith.

Every seed has an innate, God-given power and ability to give life and grow into the exact genera, or species, it was created to be. An acorn will always produce an oak tree, and an apple seed will always grow up into an apple tree, each seed producing fruit after its own kind. A tiny apple seed has the ability to grow into a tree of twenty-five to thirty feet in height and adorn itself with long branches and beautiful green leaves. It then begins the process of completing what it was created to do, and that is to produce delicious and nutritious apples. You never have to tell it to produce apples because that is what it was created to do. To be sure, the more the tree is pruned, fertilized, and watered, the healthier it will be and the more fruit it will produce. Do you see where this is going?

WORDS WILL DETERMINE YOUR FUTURE

When you come to the realization that your words are actually seeds that contain the power to produce "death or life," you will at the same time realize that God has given you, and you alone, dominion over your future. No person, no circumstance, no happenstance, no anything can keep you from being all that God has designed you to be. The enemy of darkness has known all along that God has given you Kingdom rights that empower you to conquer and overcome with words, and because of this, he has done everything in his power to keep this truth hidden from you. He has failed again because you now have revelation knowledge that your words will determine your future.

Now that you have received this revelation, your responsibility is to learn the promises of God and begin speaking them into existence in obedience to the voice of the Holy Spirit. The more you speak God's words and promises, the easier it will become to enjoy and live an abundant life. Don't get alarmed or discouraged when, from time to time, you find yourself allowing your flesh to use your mouth to speak words that are anything but what you desire or intended. Simply rebuke them, then tell your Heavenly Father you are sorry, and begin to again speak life. When your spouse or a loved one says something negative, ask them, "Do you want me to agree with that?" They will soon get the message and can then learn to do the same thing for you. It really helps!

It's easy to believe that Jesus had all power and that life emanated from His voice because we can read the accounts of His miracles in the Scriptures. You can see with great clarity that He not only walked in authority, but He spoke with authority and saw the results of His spoken words. Again, that's easy for us to believe because He was, is, and forevermore shall be "The Son of God." Dear reader, I realize that you are not "the" Son of God, but you are a beloved son or daughter, adopted into His family by the blood of Jesus. Therefore, He has endued you with the same Holy Spirit that clothed and empowered Jesus. This is not some diluted or lesser power, but the same dynamic, life-giving, life-changing power that can overcome every challenge of life.

Peter and John were privileged to be among the chosen disciples of Jesus, but without the power of the Holy Spirit living in them, they were just ordinary men. God's plan was to fill them with power, and He did exactly that. After His resurrection, Jesus appeared to His disciples, breathed on them, and said, *"Receive the Holy Spirit"* (John 20:22). He did the same thing for you when you were saved. Every born-again child of God has been baptized into the body of Christ (1 Corinthians 12:13).

Peter and John were not only baptized into the body of Christ, they were also baptized with the Holy Spirit at

Pentecost and endowed with power. Being full of the Spirit, they were on their way to the temple to pray when they encountered a lame man lying by the gate begging for alms. This man had been lame his entire life, but because of the boldness of Peter, this lame man's life was about to be changed forever. Peter said to him, *"... In the name of Jesus Christ the Nazarene—walk"* (Acts 3:6). Had Peter ignored the prompting of the Holy Spirit to speak to the lame man, or if he had allowed the image of the man's lame legs to exalt itself above the Spirit, nothing would have happened that day. They didn't have any money with them, but even if they had, money would not have changed this man's pitiful condition. Kind words and a pat on the head might have given him a momentary encouragement, but these words wouldn't have changed him, only the words of life spoken in faith were able to change him from a cripple to a healthy walking man.

You have been given the same delegated authority to use the name of Jesus and see words spoken in faith manifest themselves and become reality. The power is in you, but it's not you; it is the power of the Holy Spirit. Paul said, *"I can do all things through Him who strengthens me"* (Philippians 4:13), and so can you. Now, let's take this truth one step further, to where, as we would say, "the rubber meets the road."

It is of extreme importance for you to understand that the Spirit who lives in you must have your cooperation in order to use your mouth, your hands, and your feet, or nothing will ever happen. Mark 11:23, *"Truly I say to you, whoever says to this mountain, 'Be taken up and cast into the sea,' and does not doubt in his heart, but believes that*

whatever he says is going to happen, it will be granted him."
Take careful note of what it did *not* say; it did not say to
speak to God about the mountain. Peter did not do that
with this individual that day. He did not pray and ask God
to please heal the lame man. No, he spoke directly to the
problem in the name of Jesus because he understood that
Jesus actually healed this person when He received the
thirty-nine stripes on His body and carried them to the
Cross. *"... by His stripes we are healed"* (Isaiah 53:4-5). This
is no longer future. It's already done. Your healing has
already been paid for (see Matthew 8:16-17).

If this is too much of a stretch for you to receive or
comprehend at this time, at least be willing to allow yourself
to be a cherry picker and take what you can. But know this,
the healing for every type and kind of sickness was paid for
in full as part of Christ's atonement on the Cross. That is
Truth! Yet, this is also true: A blessing you are not sure
belongs to you cannot be claimed by faith. God's enormous
power can only be claimed in faith when it is fully known
by you that it is also His will! It was said of Jesus when He
returned to His home city of Nazareth, *"And He did not do
many miracles there because of their unbelief"* (Matthew
13:58; Mark 6:5). He was willing, but their unbelief stole
their blessing. Dear reader, their doubt does not belong to
you. In faith, the seed of knowledge concerning God's will
to heal has now been planted deep into your heart and soul.
In due time, it will produce healing and life.

You, too, have been given the authority to speak to the
mountain in the Father's name. God is the power that will
cause it to happen, but it won't happen unless you are
obedient and willing to speak to your mountains. Then,

having done all, your job is to "stand!" Not just stand and hope something changes, but to "stand guard" over what you have declared and decreed. The term "whoever" most assuredly includes you and every other born again believer. You have both the power and authority to speak life into your marriage, into a broken relationship, finances, sickness, and disease. Whatever your mountain or mountains may be, God's promises spoken in faith will cause them to be shaken, changed, moved or removed, giving you total victory.

The words you speak in faith always carry with them the power to change the improbable and to achieve the impossible because God is the Guarantor of His Word. When you don't see an immediate manifestation, refuse to be moved and do what? Stand in Faith, guarding diligently the words and promises spoken because your words are seeds of life that will not return void.

A TIME TO PLANT

"There is an appointed time for everything. And there is a time for every event under heaven … a time to plant, and a time to uproot what is planted" (Ecclesiastes 3:1-2).

Life is full of seasons, and, depending on who you ask, the number of seasons may vary. Some say three or five, others seven, and some will even say ten. There may or may not be an exact number that could be extracted from Scripture that would validate each position, but that is really missing the point. The point is that God wants you to discern when a new season is at hand and when it has ended. Without spiritual discernment, you may find yourself trying to speak life into something that God wants you to uproot and discard.

How can you know when a season is ending and a new one is beginning? First and foremost, you can learn this by reading the Word of God and searching the Scriptures. Secondly, you can know by discernment, and a part of this is learning to recognize the voice of God. His voice always has a purpose, a plan for your present time in life, as well as a plan for your future. These two truths are stand-alones, but they will always bear witness of one another. If they do not, then it's time to stop, look, and listen. There are times when God's silence is His way of saying, "Wait. The plan is okay, but the timing is not." Many people have missed out on God's best by not waiting for His timing and allowing Him to open closed doors. Others have missed the will of God by failing to move on once a season has ended.

Let the Word of God be clear. Marriage has its seasons, but it's not God's will for it to end until the appointed time of death comes for a husband or a wife. God is the spiritual glue, the third cord of marriage that binds a man and a woman together as one. He wants a husband and wife to share the journey together, step by step, day by day, year by year, till death, and death alone, ends this three-corded covenant. That is not, however, the way a lot of marriages end, so we will look for more clarification concerning marriage, separation, and divorce in Chapter Six.

For now, let's remain focused and look at five different seasons of a great marriage. If you know of more, then great; embrace and make the most of them.

1. There is a time for a husband and wife to come together, enjoy each other, become best friends, and establish an enduring marriage founded on love and respect. This is a very important season to enjoy and to use

as a time for building a solid foundation for the future.

2. There is a season in most marriages to bear children; a time to nurture and train them to love God and others as they observe the selfless love of a mother and a father.

3. There is a season when children will come of age and begin seeking their God-given vocations as they begin to move from under their parents' authority. Genesis 2:24 says, *"For this cause a man shall leave his father and his mother, and be joined to his wife; and they shall become one flesh."* God's plan and design is that there can be only one captain of every ship, one head over each family.

4. There is a time to enjoy the fruit of your labor, a time to nurture your children, your grandchildren, and when so blessed, your great grandchildren. Ask any Jesus-loving grandparent about their grandchildren, the true fruit of the vine, and they will take endless time to show you their pictures and tell you how truly grand they really are.

5. There is a time to make sure your house is in order, that a will is in place, and your last wishes concerning your estate and loved ones have been made known. You need to appoint a good, faithful, trustworthy steward that will carry out your last wishes. It would be wise to counsel with your spouse and loved ones and not let your departure be a time of confrontation and unrest.

Unless Jesus calls His Church out first, everyone will have an encounter with death, but it is not scriptural to believe that sickness must precede death. Ecclesiastes does not list sickness as having an appointed time, and neither should God's children. Talk with God about your appointed time and ask Him to allow you to fall into an eternal sleep and wake up in His presence.

TOO LATE TO GO BACK?

It's never too late to give God control of your life and allow Him to help you move forward, but at times it can be too late to go back and salvage things in the past. There is a consequence to some of our actions, and there are decisions that can become irrevocable. That is what prayer is for—to seek the Lord and allow Him to direct your path going forward. He will tell you when it's possible go back and correct things that happened in your past, and, likewise, He will tell you when it's time to stop looking back and move forward. It may be time to uproot and move into another season, but be sure you are listening to the voice of God and not strange voices. A strange voice may say "stay" when you should go, or "go" when you should stay, but you can always discern when it's a strange voice whispering in your ear and not the voice of the Holy Spirit. Only the Holy Spirit can give your heart and soul complete peace when a decision must be made.

Peace is what Christ yearns to give you in the fullest measure, but your peace will never be complete as long as you have offense or unforgiveness in your heart. As long as there is the breath of life in you or the other person, it's never too late to tell them you're sorry and to ask for forgiveness. It may be that someone has hurt you, but the same rule applies. You can't allow an offence to darken your heart and rule over your future. Forgive them and pray for them, God will take care of the rest. Forgiving others or asking for forgiveness may or may not restore a marriage, business, or a broken relationship, but it will restore your soul. A soul at peace with the Lord is in a most excellent place, and it will allow the Father to cause all things to work together for good (Romans 8:28).

PRAY RIGHT

A common prayer request of people with relationship challenges is that God will supernaturally cause another person to love them, especially when they have encountered separation or divorce. I'm sorry, but those who have ears to hear need to receive the truth concerning this matter. Praying for God to make someone love you or anyone else is not biblical. If the Kingdom of God operated that way, then Jesus could have simply prayed to the Father to change the hearts of the Pharisees toward Him. He would have prayed to the Father for them to love and accept Him as the Light of the world. But He did not, and the Pharisees did not acknowledge Him for who He was. Instead, He refused to take offence and loved them all the way to the Cross, asking of His Father, *"... Father, forgive them; for they do not know what they are doing ..."* (Luke 23:34).

Praying that God will speak to a person's heart and give enlightenment and empowerment is biblical. There are myriads of ways that God may bring enlightenment to people you pray for. If they are willing to receive and allow Him to change their hearts, He will, but He won't force Himself into a person's heart. It's almost a certainty that you have experienced times in your life when someone you loved or trusted let you down. Everyone has. But it's also during those times that you must determine to work through the pain and not allow an offence to gain a foothold of bitterness. Your breakthrough will take place when you are obedient to God's Word and pray a blessing over the one who has hurt you. God will then take over from there.

EVEN SO

Going through hard times is not a reason for divorce. (More on this later.) Feeling unloved is not a license to be unfaithful or to look for someone else. Thinking "I'm not happy, and I deserve to be happy" doesn't qualify as a reason to break the marriage covenant. Neither are financial difficulties and the subsequent emotional hardships associated with those difficulties reasons to end a marriage. God spoke to the prophet Ezekiel and said, *"… Prophesy over these bones, and say to them, 'O dry bones, hear the word of the Lord.' Thus says the Lord God to these bones, 'Behold, I will cause breath to enter you that you may come to life.'"* Verse 10: *"So I prophesied as He commanded me, and the breath came into them, and they came to life and stood on their feet, an exceedingly great army"* (Ezekiel 37:4-5, 10).

The command to prophesy the written Word still exists for New Covenant Christians. You may not have the gift of a prophet, but you can speak God's Word and promises into someone's life or into a particular situation. At times, it may involve calling things that are not as though they are. When you are obedient to do this, the challenge is no longer confined to the natural but is then moved into the realm of the supernatural. God can then bring all of His Kingdom resources into the fight against the enemy and snatch victory from the jaws of defeat. He is listening for your voice to call upon Him. Do your part in speaking life by speaking in faith and believing that the mountain will move.

God will never tell you to prophesy anything that cannot be validated by His written Word. He will never ask you to seek divorce when there are no spiritual grounds for divorce. He will never direct you to marry an unbeliever. He will never tell you to write a check that you know will be insufficient, and He will never tell you to spend money you don't have. God will never give you permission to break any of His Laws or Commandments, even though you are no longer under the power of the Law. Instead, He empowers you to live and keep them, and if you fail, He will continue to bathe you in abundant Grace.

A TIME TO REAP

Farmers plant seeds because they expect to reap a harvest. A good farmer is diligent to ensure that he has good seeds, seeds he can depend on to germinate, take root, and in time, bear fruit. Having placed them into the ground, he knows that he must continue to be diligent over what he has planted, making sure they have sufficient fertilizer and water, and when weeds appear, he is also diligent to remove them from his field.

In the same way, your words are seeds sown to create whatever you desire to take place in your life. As a child of God, you are now becoming more aware of the words you are speaking because you know they are actually supernatural seeds with the power to give life and abundance or lack and loss. Once you pray, speak, and decree God's Word into a situation, it then becomes your responsibility to be the watchman, to continuously water and fertilize the seed, making sure that the weeds don't come up unnoticed. How do you do that? By continuously praising and thanking God in advance for what He is doing. You continue to pray words of affirmation, not going back and asking again and again for the same thing, for that is not faith. You can't read or hear this too many times. Your part is to continue to stand on the promises of God until you see the manifestation.

The most common mistake of many believers is to allow doubt and fear to take control whenever there is not an immediate manifestation of whatever it is that they prayed and made request for. This waiting phase is when the enemy will do everything in his power to steal the Word from you. Satan will use his age-old ploy to focus your attention on the problem, and it's not uncommon for the mountain to appear larger and more daunting as the enemy takes his best shots at your faith and willingness to stand. The facts may seem to get worse and the problem larger, but He can only be successful if he can get you to come into agreement with the problem and speak words of doubt and unbelief.

James warned the Church, "... *the tongue is set among our members as that which defiles the entire body, and sets on fire the course of our life, and is set on fire by hell*" (James 3:6). James, the half-brother of Jesus and a leader in the early Church, is saying that our words will direct whatever goes on in our lives, whether life or death. Seeds dug up by words of unbelief will never produce the crop they were intended to produce. There is a reason that Paul exclaimed to the Church at Ephesus, "... *and having done everything, to stand firm*" (Ephesians 6:13).

It is not uncommon for doubt and fear to attack your emotions and senses. Everyone, without exception, will at various times be forced to fight those battles because it's the only place the enemy can attack a believer. Jesus defeated Satan in the unseen spiritual world, but he is still *"the prince of the power of the air"* (this world) (Ephesians 2:2). He knows that his power is limited to *"the sons of disobedience,"* or the unsaved, but he also knows that he can successfully attack those believers who don't know the Word of God or how the Kingdom of God operates. Based on what you have learned thus far, you do know how the Kingdom of God operates, and you also know that Jesus stripped Satan of his authority and that he no longer has any power or authority over you.

James said to the Church, *"Submit therefore to God. Resist the devil and he will flee from you"* (James 4:7). Don't be afraid of Satan. He cowers at the name of Jesus. And don't allow your words to dig up your seed. In due time, it will give you an abundant harvest.

Chapter 6

Marriage,
A Covenant of Three

"For this cause a man shall leave his father and mother and shall cleave to his wife; and they shall become one flesh"
(Genesis 2:24)

Marriage was God's idea, and it was a really super, wonderful idea! Seeing that Adam was alone and lonely, God performed an experiential, supernatural surgery that changed his life forever. After giving him a Holy Spirit dose of anesthetics, the Bible records that Adam fell into a deep sleep. The Master Physician then took a rib from his side and fashioned a woman. Ladies, you may want to take note here: The Bible is specific in its wording. God created, or formed (depending on the translation), Adam from the dust (plain old dirt) of the ground, but not so for the woman. He "fashioned" Eve from a rib. Is that God's way of saying that the woman is elevated, to be protected, admired, and honored? Yes, that is exactly what He was saying!

The Apostle Peter confirmed this in his letter to the Church, *"You husbands in the same way, live with your wives in an understanding way, as with someone weaker, since she is a woman ..."* (1 Peter 3:7). Most husbands need to gain the revelation that God is not referring to physical strength when He calls the woman the weaker vessel. Rather, He is reminding the husband of the delicate and amazingly intricate way his wife was created. We know the passage is not just a reference to physical strength because there are a small percentage of wives who possess greater physical strength than their husbands. Therefore, the idea that God is referring to physical strength alone must be eliminated. The Word of God is not just correct most of time; it is correct all of the time and in every situation. There are no exceptions.

Consider this: Eve was fashioned from a rib, while man was created from the dirt of the ground. This is like comparing a common plate purchased at Walmart or Target to the finest plate of China that can be purchased only at a Neiman Marcus or Tiffany's. While they both accomplish what they were designed for, one is far more delicate and subject to damage than the other. Husbands, take notice!

Peter went on to say in verse seven, *"... and show her honor as a fellow heir of the grace of life, so that your prayers will not be hindered."* The following is an understatement: "No husband can afford to have his prayers hindered." That does not mean that God is turning prayers off and on based on how good a husband treats his wife, but the atmosphere of the home can sure go downhill in a hurry when anger and selfish words are released. No husband can have confidence before the Lord if he is not in harmony with his wife. It's impossible.

God not only fashioned Eve from a rib taken from Adam's side, He also presented Eve to her future husband and proceeded to perform the very first marriage ceremony. God was, in essence, the High Priest and best man combined, and because He was the third person, marriage became a lifelong covenant between Himself and a man and woman. Get the picture: Marriage in the eyes of God is between a man and a woman. It's not to be confused with a contract and, most certainly, not to be confused with same-sex "marriage." God very plainly calls homosexuality a sin in both the Old Covenant and the New Covenant (Leviticus 18:22; 1 Corinthians 6:9-10). It is grave error to confuse God's love and patience toward a lost sinner or a saved person trapped by strongholds as being acceptance or tolerance of sin. The Cross of Jesus is proof positive that God is intolerant of sin. Nevertheless, we do not want to be guilty of grading sin. Homosexuality is no greater sin in the eyes of God than adultery, lying, or even the things that can't be seen, such as unforgiveness. There is no little sin in the eyes of God, although it is important to point out that some sins can have far greater consequences than others. One thing is for sure, God never stops loving and pursuing the lost sinner.

Marriage between a man and a woman was God's idea, and He hasn't changed His mind about it. Make no mistake, God is the Guarantor and Guardian of His covenants and promises, and He zealously watches over them. A marvelous illustration of how God meets the needs of His covenant children is recorded in the Gospel according to John beginning in chapter two. It's no coincidence that Jesus performed His very first miracle at a wedding feast that took place in Cana of Galilee.

NEED A MIRACLE?

Imagine if you were the father or mother of a newly married bridegroom. A beautiful wedding has just taken place, and the invited guests are gathering to pay tribute to the groom and his new bride. The festivities are ready to begin when, suddenly, you are told that the caterer has failed to show up with the food and drinks. Facing the bride and groom would be embarrassing enough, but how could you face their friends and guests? This would be very embarrassing to anyone, but to a Jewish family living during the time when Jesus walked here on earth, such an event would have been more than embarrassing. It would have been devastating. Such were the events taking place at this gala celebration at Cana of Galilee.

John 2:2-11 records that on the third day, a wedding feast was underway, and the customary or traditional festivities of a Jewish wedding were taking place. After days of celebrating, usually seven, it was the Jewish custom for the Father of the bridegroom to call together everyone in attendance at the celebration—family, friends, and other invited guests—and in unison they would all parade ceremoniously down the streets to the home of the betrothed. In excited anticipation, the bride and her family would wait for the expected arrival of the bridegroom. As soon as they heard the noise of the coming caravan, someone would cry out, "Behold, the bridegroom cometh!" The bridegroom would then take his betrothed wife and parade back to his home with the entire entourage in attendance.

Jesus, along with His mother and His disciples, found themselves in a similar setting, and it was at this wedding where Jesus performed His first miracle. It needs to be repeated, nothing is ever happenstance when God is involved. This unusual miracle validated His Father's will to show once again that He is very desirous of being the abundant supplier for every marriage, regardless of the need. Good news! God hasn't changed His mind or gone to plan B. He still wants to be the vital third strand in marriage that keeps it intact and vibrant, with every need fully and abundantly met.

You have probably noticed that real life is not the same as that portrayed in movies or make-believe fiction. Real life is filled with measureable moments of laughter and tears, as well as joys and sorrows. Light bills have to be paid, groceries must be purchased, clothes for growing children are a constant need, and it was the same with this Jewish family. This was real life, and the parents of the bridegroom had run out of wine. Nothing could have been more embarrassing in Jewish society than running out of wine during a wedding feast. Imagine the headline news of the *Cana Gazette*: "Jewish Family Runs Out of Wine During Wedding Feast!" What an embarrassment! What a downer when one of the most exciting and joyful events of one's life has finally arrived and now everything appears to be unraveling.

Have you ever needed a miracle? If you haven't, you will, and in this wonderful story, God wants to teach you an important lesson. When you find yourself in need of a miracle, look up, pray up, and, in faith, receive your miracle. This Jewish family desperately needed a miracle, and the God of miracles supplied them with one. He wants to do the same for you. You may not need wine, but whatever you have need of, our Lord Jesus is more than willing to supply it. How can you be assured of having your needs met?

Listen and receive these words of wisdom spoken by Mary, the mother of Jesus, "... *Whatever He says to you, do it*" (John 2:5).

Did they do as she instructed, and, if so, what were the results of their obedience?

The Bible records that there were six waterpots in the

parents' home that were used for ceremonial washing, a type of religious rite performed by many Jewish families. It was more than just the washing of one's hands if they were dirty. This Law of the Pharisees required a second washing after the first one because they believed that works and rituals were pleasing to God. In truth, it was a self-imposed rite of the Pharisees that did not please God in the least. These were not ordinary waterpots. They were huge water-pots that held about twenty to thirty gallons each. We read in verse 7: *"Jesus said to them, 'Fill the waterpots with water.' So they filled them up to the brim."* How often do we miss out on God's best by half-heartedly doing the task given to us? To the servant's credit, they gave Him their best and filled them all to the brim.

Why did God make a point of letting us know the exact number of waterpots? It is because six is the number of man. It is intended to show the utter futility of man's attempt to cleanse himself from sin.

Jesus transformed the water into the tastiest of New Wine. He could also have changed rocks into bread when he was tempted by the Devil. What was the difference in these two events? Turning water into wine was pleasing to the Father, but turning stones into bread would have been an act of yielding to the temptation called "the pride of life."

Jesus can easily turn water into wine, and He can also transform a lifeless marriage into one that is vibrant and alive. You may consider the situation to be hopeless, but that is the time when Jesus is at His best. No matter what the condition or the circumstances may be, trust in Jesus; be obedient to His voice and He will do the impossible. No one can unscramble a scrambled egg, but Jesus can. No one

Chapter 6: Marriage, A Covenant of Three

can tame the tongue (James 3:8), but Jesus can. No one can bring life to a dead marriage, but Jesus can. *"Trust in the Lord with all your heart and do not lean on your own understanding"* (Proverbs 3:5).

NOTE: For the purpose of separating the Old Covenant of Law with the New Covenant of Grace, Jesus said that man does not put New Wine into old wineskins. He also used wineskins to remind us that *tirosh*, unfermented wine, will, in time, become *yayin*, fermented, when it is allowed much time to age. Jesus created New Wine.

WHAT ABOUT DIVORCE?

This subject is important because many people who read this book have suffered the agony of divorce. If you have not divorced, you know people who have.

Concerning divorce, we find that Jesus, once again, becomes a stumbling block to the Jews and a thorn in the side of the Pharisees by confirming His Father's will that marriage is to be esteemed as a covenant, not a contract. The Pharisees conveniently reminded Jesus that the Law of Moses allowed a husband to write a certificate of divorce to his wife if he found any indecency in her. Was that God's will? No, that was never God's will, but, in patience and mercy, He withheld judgment and allowed Israel to do many things that were not His will. King David and King Solomon had many wives, and God did not count it against them.

When Jesus came on the scene, He began to set the record straight. The Law of Moses was written in stone, but the new law of Liberty is written on our hearts, and God has now made His perfect will known to us concerning marriage and divorce. Depending on where you gather statistics, the current divorce rate has risen steadily and now approaches an astounding fifty percent. That is not even taking into account the alarming rise of live-in partners who separate and go their own ways.

Jesus set the record straight and referred them back to the standard set by His Father. Jesus said to them, *"... Have you not read that He who created them from the beginning made them male and female, and said, 'For this reason a man shall leave his father and mother and be joined to his wife, and the two shall become one flesh'?"* Yes, they had heard it before, but the truth concerning marriage was not what they really wanted to hear. Very often, truth is neither convenient nor appeasing. But Jesus is not a politician, and it is evident that He was not attempting to appease the religious Pharisees. Jesus was separating truth from error. *He continued by saying, "So they are no longer two, but one flesh. What therefore God has joined together, let no man separate"* (Matthew 19:4-7).

The ears of the Pharisees were already red hot, but Jesus wasn't finished with them. He not only wanted them to hear the truth, He was desirous that they hear the whole truth and nothing but the truth, so He continued, *"... Because of your hardness of heart Moses permitted you to divorce your wives; but from the beginning it has not been this way."* He concluded by saying, *"And I say to you, whoever divorces his wife, except for immorality, and marries another woman commits adultery"* (Matthew 19:8-9).

WOW! THIS IS DEEP WATER!

The questions could then be asked, "What about the millions who have divorced their spouses when adultery was not an issue? What about them? What about those who were unfaithful to their marriage partners and caused divorce to take place? Are they eternally convicted and condemned for their decision to divorce?" Most importantly, "Is this an unpardonable sin?" The answer is an emphatic, "No!"

FOR GRACE HAS APPEARED

Early on in my Christian walk, my wife and I attended a Sunday School class that we both loved and enjoyed. We loved the teacher, and we loved the others who were a part of the class. They loved us as well. Occasionally, the topic of divorce would arise, especially when these Scriptures were being read, and there was always an instant feeling of discomfort that permeated the air because my wife and I both came from backgrounds of divorce. People who had never suffered divorce were equally discomforted. No one's eyes met with any others because the stern, truthful words of Jesus sounded final. They seemed to say, "Guilty," without recourse.

Here is the difficulty in which we and millions of others find ourselves with the mixture of Law and Grace. Is it sin to divorce and break the Covenant Law of Marriage when a partner has not been unfaithful? The answer is, "Yes." Jesus Himself confirmed that the breaking of the marriage covenant without cause of unfaithfulness is sin. But does this mean that divorce is an unpardonable sin? The answer is, "No." The Law still condemns it, and divorce is still a travesty, but we are no longer under the Law. We now live under Grace.

This great truth bears repeating often, "We now live under Grace." The cold reality is this: Without grace, sin would not only keep us from entering heaven, but all of humanity would be denied entrance as well. Thanks be to God, we aren't without grace. Paul proclaimed, *"... where sin increased, grace abounded all the more"* (Romans 5:20).

Once again, because this truth is so important: From a literary view, the Old Covenant ended with the last words of the prophet Malachi, and the New Covenant began with the first page of Matthew. But from a doctrinal view, the Old Covenant was still in place when Jesus preached the Sermon on the Mount and when He confronted the Jews concerning divorce. The Old Covenant ended on the Cross with these words, *"It is finished."* Jesus fulfilled the Old Covenant on the Cross, thereby making it obsolete (Hebrews 8:13). The New Law of Liberty was established when the power of God raised His Son Jesus from the dead and seated Him at His right hand in heaven. Sin and death no longer have dominion or strongholds over the children of God. The New Law makes you complete in Christ, no matter how long or egregious your previous sin record is. How can this be? By the redemptive, shed blood of Jesus!

"'Come now, and let us reason together,' says the Lord, 'though your sins are as scarlet, they will be as white as snow; though they are red like crimson, they will be like wool'" (Isaiah 1:18).

Isaiah was prophesying a future event we can now see with much greater clarity on our side of the Cross than on his. He was looking at an event that had yet to take place, while we are looking with awe and wonder at an event that has already taken place. The Cross and the Resurrection of Jesus from death and the grave changed everything. Therefore, let you and me reason together as well.

Consider Abraham, who lied not once but twice about his true relationship with his wife Sarah. He purposely and selfishly instructed her to tell others that she was his sister, not his wife, and allowed her to be taken into the homes of lustful men of prestige, power, and authority in order to save himself. To say that Abraham was not perfect is an understatement, but God still counted him as righteous and chose him to be the Father of a mighty nation, calling him the friend of God.

Moses had an anger problem, so much so that it caused him to murder a man when he was a prince in Egypt.

Consider another man, an adulterer and a murderer, a man we know as King David. Under Old Testament Law, God judged him for his acts of sin but continued to bless his life, calling him a man after His own heart.

Sampson was a Levite and judge over Israel who not only committed adultery, but willfully broke many of the Levite Laws and spurned the known will of God for his life.

Saul was a zealous Pharisee who ravaged the Christian Church and killed many of them. He later became known as the Apostle Paul.

The list goes on and the word "sin" can easily be attached to each and every one of them. It is interesting to note that although all of the men previously mentioned are named in the Book of Hebrew's Faith Hall of Fame, there is amazingly no reference to their sin. That is because Grace has now triumphed over Law, and the blood of Jesus has eradicated their sins forever.

The fact that society at large no longer connects divorce to sin, regardless of the reason, doesn't change the words of Jesus. His word endures forever, but thanks be unto Him,

He is also our God of mercy. In mercy, grace has appeared, bringing salvation to all men. Now, all of our sins, past, present, and future, have been paid for in full, and that, dear reader, is inclusive of divorce. How great is our salvation!

WANT A GREAT MARRIAGE?
HOW DOES IT HAPPEN?

Communication. This is said to be the key to having a great marriage. This is always at the top of the list for wives.

Sex. This one is generally at or near the top of the list for men.

Finances. It has often been said that this is the one that broke the camel's back.

Flip a switch and get happy? Never get upset again? Take an anger control course? Get rid of the old jalopy and purchase a new car? Move into a nicer home? Go on exotic vacations? Shop in the high-end stores for all of your clothes? Finally, catch up to the Jones family? Nope, that's not how, and if the list were longer and had more pet peeves, it still wouldn't be the way to build an exciting and wonderful marriage.

HERE'S HOW

1. *"Wives, be subject to your own husbands, as to the Lord"* (Ephesians 5:22; 1 Peter 3:1).

2. *"Husbands, love your wives, just as Christ also loved the church and gave Himself up for her"* (Ephesians 5:25; 1 Peter 3:7).

God gave only two directives for your marriage to flourish and become a wonderful, supernatural, great marriage. While the subjects mentioned previously are important and beneficial for enjoying a healthy marriage, such as communication, sex, financial success, etc., they are merely the fruit, not the root, of marital success. The Lord gave only two commandments for a successful marriage, one to the man, and one to the woman. Embrace these, learn what they mean, and you will have a most wonderful, supernatural marriage.

WIVES

"Wives, be subject to your own husbands, as to the Lord" (Ephesians 5:22; 1 Peter 3:1).

Let's begin with you, wives. Society would have you believe that being subject to your husband is a subservient demand that makes you unequal to your husband and is therefore demeaning and condescending. Nothing could be farther from the truth. God has already revealed how highly He esteems the woman, so you know with certainty that you are not less important than your husband. You would not see yourself as demeaned or unequal if you boarded an airplane or ship and saw the captain in his place of authority over the crew, and not only over the crew but over the passengers as well. On the contrary, you would probably disembark if there was no captain in charge of the ship or plane.

No, it is not that God esteems a husband as being more important than a wife, for there is no partiality with Him. It's all about the fact that God has equipped your husband to protect, provide for, and guide you and your family through the journey of life. If that is not currently the case, and it seems there is no captain in charge, then read on because God knows how to turn your husband into a real man. Right now, he is not the focus or the issue; you are.

Notice that God did not say that you are to be subject to your husband only when he is behaving in a wonderful and loving way. It said to be subject to him as you are subject to your Lord. You don't pick and choose when you want to be subject to the Lord, and you shouldn't pick and choose when you will be subject to your husband. On the flip side, it did not say that you are to be subject to your husband if he asks you to do anything that is immoral or unethical because God will never ask you to do anything immoral or unethical. Neither does God expect you or your children to live in an abusive home. If that is where you find yourself, pray and ask God for direction. He will guide you.

Dear wife, God understands that your husband is not a carbon copy of His Son Jesus, and He fully understands that there are times when he carries little or no resemblance to Jesus. God is omniscient, knowing all things, and He wants you to realize that your obedience will allow Him to open doors that your husband has closed. With your help, He can move more quickly to help your husband become the shining man of God he was created to be.

Proverbs 14:1: *"The wise woman builds her house, but the foolish tears it down with her own hands."* A more general way of saying this is: "A wise woman builds a beautiful marriage by honoring her husband with both her words and her actions, while a foolish woman destroys her home and marriage by doing exactly the opposite."

Let's be clear. You can't change your husband, but you

can be a most wonderful and positive influence in his life. Remember, God created your husband from plain old dirt, so he thinks differently than you. He thinks nothing of drinking milk from a gallon jug or acting in an uncouth manner. There is a reason he is challenged to eat a meal without dropping food on his shirt or putting colors together when he dresses. Wives, it's really true, most husbands don't have the ability to keep up with several subjects at the same time as you have been gifted to do, so when you ask him what he is thinking and he says nothing, he's probably telling you the truth. Ask him about a meeting or event, and rest assured he will sum it up in just a few words. Yes, God knows that you want the specific details, but learn to ask for more details without getting frustrated and upset. He was created from plain old dirt.

Are there areas where you can help your husband improve? Yes, there are many areas in which you can help him improve, but God alone has the power and ability to change the inner man. Sound hopeless? It's not, and you can take heart in the knowledge that God, in His great wisdom, created your husband with an intuitive ability to love, protect, and provide for your physical and emotional needs, as well as the needs of your family. Hopefully, your husband is already fulfilling his role as the spiritual leader of your home, but if he isn't, sit back and enjoy watching the Holy Spirit work in his heart as you continue to love and respect him as God instructed you to do.

Your part is to lift him up in both words and actions before others, especially your children. He is equipped to fight the world and do quite well, but continuous negative words from his wife are too heavy for him to carry. In time,

Great Life, Great Marriage

the weight of negative words will bring him to his knees and, over a period of time, will end up filling him with resentment. Make it your goal to become his best friend, one whom he is always willing to come to and confide in, a wife he enjoys spending time with. That will never happen if you are constantly nagging and making demands that he isn't comfortable doing, even well-meaning requests like reading his Bible, praying, or going to church. You can, however, take his hand and pray for him and over him. Pray in love, calling things that are not as though they are by speaking prophetically that he is a good husband and leader, that he is a special father and example to his children. But don't demand that he be the spiritual leader when he isn't ready to assume the role.

Many wives have failed to heed these words of wisdom and unwittingly opened doors of strife and resentment to the enemy. On the other hand, by taking the alternative course of continually speaking and praying God's promises and blessings over your husband, you will have the opposite effect. Praying and confessing God's promises will most assuredly usher in joy, peace, and contentment because God watches over His Word to perform it. Pray in faith for your husband and refuse to be moved by his negative actions or words. Pray and believe in your heart that he is becoming the spiritual leader and man of God that you and your children so desperately want him to be.

Is this a guarantee for success? No, it's not a guarantee. Your husband may never change, but your obedience to honor and respect his God-given position as leader of your home is a guarantee that God will bring His supernatural power into the equation. In those moments of time, God

118

will deal with his heart as only He can and help him make positive spiritual decisions concerning his actions and behavior. Believe God, love God, and trust God with your husband. *"Love never fails ..."* (1 Corinthians 13:8).

HUSBANDS

"Husbands, love your wives, just as Christ also loved the church and gave Himself up for her" (Ephesians 5:25; 1 Peter 3:7).

Gentlemen, the command given to our wives is difficult, but it doesn't take a rocket scientist to understand that the command given to husbands is equally as difficult, if not more so. It's not only a difficult command, but it's an impossible command to accomplish by the will of the flesh. However, man of God, you are not in the flesh but in the Spirit, and with the power of the Spirit at work, doing what the Heavenly Father is requiring of you is a piece of cake (Romans 8:9).

Loving your wife is a choice. Loving your wife as Christ loved the Church is also a choice, but it brings the love factor to an entirely different level, a level so high that you can only attain it through surrender and dying to self. Christ did not have a conditional or a passive love because those adjectives are not really love at all. Real love is always active, alive, passionate, and saturated with humility and long-suffering.

God declares this great spiritual truth in Philippians 1:6, *"For I am confident of this very thing, that He who began a good work in you will perfect it until the day of Christ Jesus."*

Allow me to share a perfect example of this Scripture in action. I was leaving a men's Bible study early one morning when a young man who loves the Lord and was excited about his Christian faith followed me out to my vehicle. He shared with me that God was dealing with him about being abrupt and short with his soon-to-be bride. I pointed out to him that most men become short tempered and abrupt when someone trespasses onto their territory, but I also reminded him that the continuous work of the Holy Spirit is to teach, reprove, correct, and train him for success in life and marriage (2 Timothy 3:16). I encouraged him to ask God for grace to be more thoughtful and gentle, and to share what God was doing in his heart with his soon-to-be wife. Husbands, there is tremendous cleansing power available when we are willing to humble ourselves and, at times, to share our weaknesses with our wives. Like our loving Father, they already know our weaknesses all too well, but their love will be strengthened by our humility, and so will we.

NOW, A QUICK CHECK-UP

Let's take a look at some of the weaknesses and heart issues that God wants to deal with in husbands. It's very difficult for most men to show their emotions and express their love for others. Therefore, God wants to begin the process of strengthening your position as head of the home by softening your heart. God is not interested in self-works and your efforts to become a good leader. Rather, He is very desirous that you seek after Him with a broken and contrite heart.

Another heart issue is to remind you that even though it's against your fleshly nature to stop and ask for directions, you need to be willing to allow Jesus to become the Lamp unto your feet and the Light unto your path. He also wants to remind you that when Jesus, the Good Shepherd, went looking for you, it wasn't because you were looking for Him. What did He find when He found and saved you? He redeemed a man who had the ability to love his wife and children conditionally but not unconditionally, not in the way that Christ loves His Church.

Thankfully, God is patient, but He is now saying to every husband and father that it's time to stand up, buckle your belt, and be the real husband and leader your wife and family need you to be. You may already be that type of man, but even if you're not, you want to improve and become the man God wants you to be or you wouldn't be reading this book. Who and what is God's type of man? God's idea of a real man is one who is well-accomplished and passes the next ten statements with ease. Take a few moments to read each statement and give yourself ten points for each one that describes your thoughts and actions toward your wife.

YOU ARE GOD'S TYPE OF A MAN IF:

1. You would never dream of hurting your wife physically and would never demean or hurt her with words. This includes telling cute jokes about her to friends. No, God's man would never do those things.

2. You open the car door for her at every opportunity and even take an extra fifteen seconds to reach over and buckle her seat belt.

3. You always send cards and flowers for special occasions and frequently even when there is no special occasion.

4. You never walk ahead of your wife when in public, even when you are in a hurry. You always keep her by your

side because you consider her to be very special, the crown of her husband, and you want her and others to know how proud you are that she is your wife and how much you love and respect her.

5. You stand when your wife comes to the dinner table and help her to be seated, and not just when there is company or on a special occasion.

6. You are willing to give up things you enjoy in order to do things with her that she sees as important. Weddings, funerals, birthdays, and other special events never seem to come at convenient times, but when they do occur, you are willing to give her your time and make yourself available with a good and joyous attitude.

7. You take her hand and pray God's promises, protection, and blessings over her each and every day.

8. You guard your eyes and don't allow them to follow other women, realizing that few things are more hurtful or demeaning to your wife and children than being untrue with your eyes.

9. You take your stand as the spiritual leader and provider of your home, making sure that you are spending daily, quality time with the Lord.

10, You love your wife unconditionally, and you would never hesitate to give your life in order to protect her.

Total your score, and take into consideration that this is not a composite list of qualities and attributes that make you a godly husband, but it is a good place to start a self-evaluation. God may be speaking to you about other areas in your life that aren't listed here, or He may be speaking to you about different things that are listed here. Regardless of your score, it goes without saying that every man, every husband, has a great deal of room for improvement.

Dear husband, no matter how you scored, God is not pointing a condemning finger at you. Rather, He is by His Spirit gently reminding you of who you are and Whose you are and of how precious your wife is. God already sees you as His man, a husband who passes this list with flying colors. He also sees you as a champion, one robed in His righteousness and full of wisdom, knowledge, and understanding.

MOVING TO A HIGHER LEVEL

So, man and woman of God, how do you move on from here and begin putting your knowledge into action? For starters, consider stopping at the foot of the Cross and allowing the redemptive blood of Jesus to begin cleansing your heart, mind, and soul. Supernatural things begin to happen when you spend time with Jesus. Your flesh will become less argumentative and far less demanding as the Holy Spirit begins to teach and empower you to love your mate more than yourself. The Holy Spirit will begin breaking the fleshly chains that have kept you in captivity and that control your moods and thoughts. He will guard your heart and soul and keep you from being offended by the words or actions of others that once kept you upset and withdrawn. To sum it up, the Holy Spirit will effortlessly make you more like Jesus, allowing you to unconditionally love your mate and say with true heartfelt emotion these life-changing words, "I love you." That's for starters, and you will find that the benefits are enormous.

Finally, allow your mind to remember a moment in time when you visited a funeral home or attended a funeral. We can agree that the person lying in the casket was totally unmoved by the activity and conversations that went on around them. That is the real meaning of dying to self. In the same way that dead people are no longer controlled or moved by other people's words or deeds, your goal is to be dead to offence and alive to things that are of good report.

CAUTION! Dying to self is not a one-time thing. I have not yet completely overcome the process, so don't get discouraged during the dying process. It will continue until God calls you unto Himself. Instead, be very much encouraged. You have not yet arrived and no one else on this side of heaven has either, but you have left the station and the journey and scenery are absolutely magnificent!

CHILDREN

Children are a great joy and blessing from the Lord, but with them comes a tremendous amount of parental responsibility. Proverbs 22:6 says, *"Train up a child in the way he should go, even when he is old he will not depart from it."* Is this an absolute? Yes, I believe it is an absolute, but I don't believe it's a slam dunk or a guarantee that children will never stray from the truth at times. Sad to say, many will. However, I am glad to say that God will never leave nor forsake them and neither will a godly parent.

One important thing to remember about your offspring is that they don't really belong to you. They belong to the Lord, and He has loaned them to you for a season. God, in His great wisdom, created the family to be the foundation of all society and, as the family goes, so goes society. Each generation brings with it values and morals that will guide the values and morals of individuals and nations. Today, the biblical, moral values of every family and nation are under severe attack because the world does not now, nor has it ever, been willing to be constrained by God's commandments.

Even though the family is under severe satanic attack, Christian parents need not be dismayed because God's love and power, along with His redemptive blood have made it possible to raise your children from cradle to adulthood and cause them to be triumphant as they go forth into the world. God's ability to change children into powerful, loving, Christian men and women are constrained only by their parents' willingness to bring them to Him.

A small child represents a new life, a life that needs to have the love of Christ instilled in its heart. As sweet and adorable as newborns are, they are all born with a sin nature. That is where moms and dads come in because, although the love of Christ and their need for a Savior can be taught, teaching is only a part of it. These things must be caught as much as taught, and it is caught by seeing love in action between a mother and a father. Taking your children to church instead of sending them with someone else is also a huge part of making sure that the love of Christ is poured into their fertile minds and souls.

Wisdom is calling loudly, so that every mom and dad can hear and receive this statement: "Going to church should never be considered to be an option in your home."

Dads, it is your responsibility to set the standard for making sure that your family has a church home that is teaching God's Word and that your entire family is involved in its activities. No exceptions. Joshua said, *"… choose for yourselves today whom you will serve … but as for me and my house, we will serve the Lord"* (Joshua 24:15). Please, do not receive this crossroads, life-changing advice as Law or as a mandate that clouds your mind with thoughts that God is not pleased if you aren't in church every time the doors are open. Instead, receive it in the way that God intended His Church to receive it, as a spiritual, life-changing decision to nurture and grow yourself, your spouse, and your children in the love and admonition of the Lord.

Every mom and dad already knows that children are created with different personalities, as well as distinct likes and dislikes. They are all unique, made special by the miracle-working creative hands of the Lord. No child is an accident. They may not have been planned, but they are not accidents. Each one is created by God with a particular plan and purpose for their lives, and it's the responsibility of every parent to help them mature and maximize their strengths while learning to minimize and overcome their weaknesses. You can do that by bathing them in prayer, praying with them, listening to them, and guiding them with biblical counsel. It would be wise to sit down with your children before they reach the age of twelve and talk with them about their salvation. It's much easier to lead them to Christ at an early age than it is as they grow older. Never force the issue, but be sure their young hearts and minds understand that they were born with a sin nature, and it is for that reason that they need a Savior.

As your children move into their teenage years, they will need more specific guidance and counsel. They will need to know that there are new parameters and guidelines that you expect them to adhere to. They will also need to know that there are consequences when they choose to disobey and step over those boundaries. One of the surest ways to allow strife and unrest to take up residence in your home is by moving on a whim the parameters you set for your children or ignoring them when they are broken. Therefore, mom and dad, you need to be in agreement about the standards and parameters you put into place for your children. You also need to be in agreement that you won't allow your children to bypass given parameters by coming to one of you individually. Confrontation is not fun, but, at times, it's very necessary.

Is spanking permissible? You decide because every child is different and will respond differently to the way they are disciplined. Proverbs 23:13-14, *"Do not hold back discipline from the child, although you strike him with the rod, he will not die. You shall strike him with the rod and rescue his soul from Sheol."* Let's look carefully at what God is saying and not read something into God's directives that isn't there.

First and foremost, the Word is saying that when your child needs to be disciplined, it is your job as their parent to do exactly that. However, this proverb is not a stand-alone directive that mandates spanking as being the only way, or even the best way, to discipline a child. In fact, spanking should be considered a last resort, not the first alternative when discipline is needed. If your child will not respond to your words or requests, then spanking may be in order, but it shouldn't be preceded by howling and becoming angry. That is the last thing they need to hear and see from their parent. Always speak in a calm voice, but be assertive in your tone. If you find you must tell your child the same thing several times to obey a command, it's your fault. Children will at times test your willingness to keep the boundary line in place, and the sooner they find that it is immovable, the more pleasant life becomes for everyone. Again, spanking may be necessary for some children, and, to be sure, it is never pleasant for either parents or children, but when it is necessary, "Use CAUTION!" Never spank a child when you are angry, and never use any object that might inflict damage to their body. Most importantly, never spank until you are in full control of your feelings and emotions.

This proverb is also telling parents that failure to discipline a child when they are young can have severe consequences for everyone when they grow older. As children move into their double digit birthdays, and in many situations sooner, it would be prudent to stop spanking as a means of discipline and begin correcting them as God corrects you, with His Word. This is not to suggest that further correction, such as a loss of privileges, is not in order, but be sure that, whatever it is, you are willing to follow through on whatever you tell them. When they are disciplined, especially when spanking is involved in their younger years, always sit down with them, give them a hug and reassure them with kind words of how much you love them and how special they are. They may draw away and want to sulk, but love in action will always win, and in due time, it will produce the desired fruit and reactions.

BLENDED FAMILIES

Today, there is an even greater challenge for many families that are labeled, "Blended Families." If you are the father or mother of a blended family, God wants you to know that your best years are still in front of you. Is your situation easy? No, but neither is it impossible. It's usually not easy because the children of divorced and remarried parents must learn to cope with a new mom or dad, and, very often, new step-brothers and sisters as well. These children are trying to deal with much more than normal growing pains. They are also dealing with the emotions of rebellion and resentment because of what they see as a loss of home security, and they now find themselves being told they must be obedient to a new mom or dad. Remember, love never fails, and it will not fail you if you find yourself in this type of situation. But it must be a love that is saturated in patience and wisdom.

Parents of blended families need to be very careful to keep a godly, healthy perspective regarding their family priorities. Dad and mom, listen closely: You must keep your relationship of husband and wife strong and intact and not allow your children to drive a wedge between you! Emotions run deep, and, at the time, they may not accept or understand some of the decisions you make for them, but in their later years, they will. For moms, this is even harder because a mother's parental instinct is to protect her child from emotional pain and hurt. Mom and dad, try to avoid making unnecessary decisions for a child that will cause friction and discord in your marital relationship. Understand each other's heart and learn to understand the heart of the child. Children who are suddenly thrust into blended family environments are not normally happy campers, but they can and will become happy campers if they are bathed in caring and compassionate love.

The reason blended families exist can be multi-faceted, but they usually exist because a dad, and in a few cases a mom, failed to provide the proper spiritual leadership and accountability in their previous marriage. If that is you, remember that you can't be successful going forward by beating yourself up about yesterday. You can't unscramble an egg, but God can. God is the absolute Master of taking bad, and at times seemingly unbearable, family situations and turning them into loving and harmonious relationships, but He needs your help. Seek the Lord for wisdom and direction daily, and He will help you train your children in the way they should go. In fact, it's a specialty of His.

There is much more that could be written about raising children, but let's close out this section with a few suggestions and things you can do to help not only your children, but their friends and loved ones as well.

1. Train your children to honor their parents and their fellow siblings with both words and deeds.

2. Train them to stand and look people in the eye when they are being introduced. Train them to say, "Yes, sir/ma'am."

3. Train them to say, "Please, May I, and Thank you." Train them to tell the truth and to accept responsibility for their actions.

4. Train them to do their best at whatever task they have, such as school work or other activities.

5. Train them to be champions by teaching them who they are in Christ, while speaking words of encouragement into them on a continual basis.

6. Train them to work when they are young, and don't forget to reward them with words, hugs, and money as they progress. You will never regret it. In return, they will grow up to be fruitful, rewarding adults whom you will always be proud of.

7. Most importantly, train them to love the Lord by setting a godly example for them.

Next, you may consider becoming a little more pro-active by helping to bring Christian men and women into your schools who can effectively speak into the lives of our young people and teenagers. Dean Sikes Ministry's "You Matter" program is one of the best. Their slogan is "Eradicating Hopelessness." Dean is a godly man who has devoted his life to speaking hope and direction to young people. He has written several books, and one of his best is a yearly devotional geared to young people and teens. It's a must-have for every teen. You can find him on the web at www.deansikes.net

Finally, let me offer up one final tip to mom and dad, but especially to dad. Always follow through and keep your word whenever you tell a child you will do something with or for them. It's easy to promise a child or teen that you will do something later when "now" is not convenient, such as the times when you are watching a game or are busy doing other things. Not following through with your promise is a big "No-No"! You must be true to your word because your word is your true character, the very thing you are trying to instill in your children.

FINANCES

The foundation of a great life and a great marriage is not built on the amount of money you possess or your financial worth, although money is important. Contrary to the teachings of many who misquote Scripture concerning money, it is not the root of all evil, and the Holy Scriptures never say that it is. Money is neither good nor evil. It's simply a tool of exchange for getting what you want or need from the person or entity who can supply that want or need. The Word of God says, "For the love of money is a root of all sorts of evil …" (1 Timothy 6:10). The "love" of money is, in reality, greed in action, and that is always a huge problem because those who love money are never satisfied with what they have, and more is never enough.

King Solomon, the wealthiest person who ever lived (his wealth was not promissory paper), gave this sage advice: *"He who loves money will not be satisfied with money, nor he who loves abundance with its income, This too is vanity"* (Ecclesiastes 5:10). He followed up with this advice. *"Do not weary yourself to gain wealth, cease from your consideration of it, When you set your eyes on it, it is gone …"* (Proverbs 23:4-5).

It is safe to say that most people, and hopefully, including you, are not in love with money. Instead, you want a sufficient amount to pay your bills, get out of debt, help others in time of need, while enjoying many of the better things in life. If that pretty much sums up your feelings, then let's look at a few basic things that will make those desires a reality in your life because the Bible has a lot to say about money.

There are natural laws that govern God's visible creation, such as seed time and harvest, with every seed producing after its own kind. There are also laws that govern electricity and gravity, things that exist but are not visible to the naked eye. There are also spiritual laws. These laws all have their beginning with God and, therefore, have dominion over everything, both that which is seen and that which is unseen, including money. All natural laws work the same for everyone, but this is not true when it comes to spiritual laws. The world has its own set of natural laws concerning wealth and money, and it is very evident that they work when you consider that much of the world's monetary wealth is owned and controlled by the unsaved. Jesus said, *"... He causes His sun to rise on the evil and the good, and sends rain to fall on the righteous and the unrighteous"* (Matthew 5:45). Why is this so? Because God loves the lost just as much as He loves the saved, and He often uses the unsaved to take care of the needs of His children.

One reason the unsaved own so much of the world's wealth can be traced back to what many pastors teach concerning money. Teachings such as "Beware" of the prosperity gospel and "a little cabin in the corner of glory land" have caused many Christians to have the wrong thoughts toward money, and, as you now know, *"... as he* [a man] *thinks within himself, so he is"* (Proverbs 23:7). To be sure, there are charlatans who dress themselves in sheep's clothing and prey upon those who are desperate for a financial miracle, but their false message should not be allowed to cancel out God's desire for His children to prosper financially. As previously noted, there is always an opportunity to love money, but that will never happen when Christ is your First Love.

When you really think about it, there are only two gospels concerning money. One is the "Prosperity Gospel," and the other is the "Poverty, or Just Enough, Gospel." Which one did Jesus preach? Jesus preached that He wants you to prosper and walk in divine health, even as your soul prospers (3 John 2). He came to save, heal, and to reveal Himself as our God of abundance. When He fed the five thousand and the four thousand, there were baskets of leftovers following each miracle. Afterward, there was not just enough to get by, but baskets full of leftovers. God is always our God of more than enough because He knows that you can't give what you do not own. You can't help the poor if you are poor yourself. You can't feed the hungry people of the world if you are anxious and worried every time you take your groceries to the check-out counter. The just enough for me mentality is really a copout that is very displeasing to our heavenly Father. Prosperous people can help others when money matters, but you can't give what you don't have, it's as simple as that.

With these thoughts in mind, let's look at some of the fiscal laws that govern God's children, never forgetting that, *"It is the blessing of the Lord that makes rich, and He adds no sorrow to it"* (Proverbs 10:22). The same cannot be said of the wealthy who are unsaved and leave God out of their finances. Their lives will always be filled with sorrow and unrest because money cannot purchase salvation, nor can it purchase peace of mind or a peaceful soul.

THE TITHE

God did not make living in prosperity difficult to achieve. In fact, He made it very simple. The Apostle Paul said, *"Now this I say, he who sows sparingly will also reap sparingly, and he who sows bountifully will also reap bountifully"* (2 Corinthians 9:6). Is this the New Covenant? It's both the Old Covenant and New Covenant because it had its beginning almost 500 years before the birth of the Old Covenants. We can easily see that the tithe was operational during the time Abraham lived, as the Bible records that he offered a tithe offering to the High Priest, Melchizedek (Genesis 14:18-20). What were the results of his obedience to the tithe? The Bible says of Abraham that he was not only rich, but that he was "very rich" (Genesis 13:2).

Today, nothing has changed concerning the tithe. It's still the seed that will cause your income to prosper. But let's be clear. God doesn't need your tithe. The lights of heaven won't blink out if you never tithe, but yours probably will because Christians live by a different set of rules than what the world lives by. God's foundational rules for His children are based on the premise of tithing— sowing and reaping. He put the tithe into place as a way to bless you, and he put the law of giving into place so that He can extravagantly bless you. But He is limited if you aren't willing to trust Him with ten percent of your income. Tithing really comes down to faith and trusting God with your financial resources. Christians who don't tithe limit God to miracles and mercy, and that isn't God's best. Financial miracles that save the day are a wonderful blessing, but learning how to walk in abundance is a lot more fun and a lot less stressful. Living in lack and stress is not conducive to living a great life and a great marriage.

"Bring the whole tithe into the storehouse, so that there may be food in My house, and test Me now in this," says the LORD *of hosts, "if I will not open for you the windows of heaven and pour out for you a blessing until it overflows. Then I will rebuke the devourer for you ..."* (Malachi 3:10-11).

Of this you can be certain, God will keep His end of the bargain because it's a part of the Covenant He made with you when you were saved. Opening the windows of Heaven and pouring out a blessing is what He has promised to do, and He will. As an added bonus, He will also rebuke the devourer so that you can walk in His divine favor. That's huge because the devourer will limit your income by causing things to break that are expensive to repair. He will keep your tires flat and your gas tank empty. Not only that, the devourer will put holes in your pockets, and when you reach in, the cupboard will be bare. If that scenario sounds familiar and you really are sick and tired of being sick and tired, then begin the change by trusting the Lord with your tithe. Just a word of advice: Give God the first check, not the amount left over after your needs and wants have been paid for.

As you learn to trust Him with the tithe, He will also enable you to be a giver because He wants to bless you even more. One thing is for certain. You can't out give God, and He will never be indebted to you. How does all of this work? It works like everything else in His Kingdom does, by obedience and faith, and true faith doesn't have a back door.

"There is one who scatters [sows]*, and yet increases all the more. And there is one who withholds what is justly due, and yet it results only in want"* (Proverbs 11:24, bracketed words added for clarity).

Knowing how God's Kingdom operates is important, but learning to trust Him and walk in obedience is equally important. Learn to live inside a budget, and do not spend more than you make. This is of paramount importance because, frequently, more money will not solve the lack problem. The lack problem is almost always solved by living inside of your current budget and income. Not that you have or would even be tempted by the lifestyle of others, but don't put your eyes on the Jones family. When you finally get to the point where you have caught up to where they live, it seems that they always end up moving to another neighborhood, and moving can be very expensive.

Put your eyes and heart on God's Word and realize that the borrower is the lender's slave. Learn to deny yourself and not live on credit. The world says that you deserve a vacation every year, but if you can't afford one, then that is a lie. Learn to walk by faith in the area of finances because the monetary resources God has set aside for your needs and desires are limitless. God will give you the wisdom to become financially free if you allow Him. It isn't all about you; it's about getting the money to you if He knows He can get it through you. Without debt, your life will be a lot more fun and a lot less stressful. Sound impossible? It's not. God wants you to live debt free.

Much more could be added to this short section on finances, but hopefully you begin to get the picture. There are great Christian materials available, such as those produced by Crown Financial Ministries, that will give you a more complete view and understanding concerning the area of money. It's a great course on finances that every husband and wife should take together. Money troubles by themselves are not the straw that breaks the camel's back. The overload began when Jesus was relegated to the co-pilot's seat.

LOVING AND LIVING

Living a great life and enjoying a super fantastic marriage is God's desire for you, so much so that He gave His Son Jesus as a living sacrifice for your salvation and your well-being. Never let any evil spirit tell you otherwise.

Become determined that, from this day forward, you will begin living the abundant life that Jesus died to give you. He died to give you salvation in eternity and an abundant life here on earth. Jesus, the Son of God, is now seated at the right hand of His Father and is anxiously waiting for you to come boldly into the throne room of grace and lay claim to your inheritance.

Will you do it? Yes, you will do it because you love the Father more than you love yourself. You will do it because it's His will for you to do it. Not only will you do it, but you will also take all that belongs to you because so many others desperately need for you to be successful.

Chapter 7

What Now???

The following is a very important and imposing question that you need to answer. *What do you intend to do with the rest of your life?*

God has left you His last will and testament, a living will, so that you can enjoy a great life and a great marriage as you continue your journey here on earth. Proverbs 13:22 says, *"A good man leaves an inheritance to his children's* children." How much more so has your heavenly Father done exactly that for you? He included you in His living will and revealed His plan and purpose for your life by making it very clear that He doesn't want you traveling streets named, "Ifida," "Wishida," and "Oneofthesedays." His design and plan is for you to walk in divine health and to prosper in every area of your life, as well as to be able to receive your covenant blessings because you already possess a prosperous soul. God has bequeathed to you everything pertaining to life and godliness, and empowered you to be more than an overcomer in every facet of your life.

Does this revelation of Christ's redemptive work mean that you have reached a place where every day is a utopia and sadness and sorrows are now non-existent? No, there is no such place here on earth, but God has provided the way for you to daily overcome every adversity and circumstance. You can overcome because you live in Him and Christ lives in you. Of this you can be certain, He will continue to take you into higher places where the supernatural always overcomes the natural, and it is in those precious moments of time that you need to pause and rest in Him. Think of the times when hope seemed to be beyond your grasp, but somehow He made a way. You will always be thankful that you made the decision to put your trust in Him, and with a thankful heart, praise Him for the enormous blessings that He has so liberally showered upon you and your loved ones.

When God impressed on me the need to write this book, He also impressed upon my heart the need to reveal His unconditional love for every living soul. This includes the saved and the lost, the just and the unjust. He who was willing to die in order to give you all things pertaining to life and godliness has promised that He will never leave nor forsake you, and He will never stop loving you. Because of this wonderful truth, you can live each day in confidence that God is no longer counting your sins and failures against you, and now realize that His blessings don't ebb and flow based on your works. Instead, they flow unabated because of the finished work of Jesus Christ on the Cross.

There are many reasons that God so richly desires for you to live a great life and enjoy a great marriage, but once again, the first and foremost of these are because you are His child, and He loves you very much. He also desires for you to become a living testimony to others because you will be the only "bible" some people will ever read. As a child of God, never allow yourself to settle for anything short of His best because He gave His best for you. You are His hands and feet, His Ambassador to the lost, and also to Christians who are clueless about how to live a victorious life here on earth, not understanding that they are "of the Kingdom."

The good things in life are worth fighting for, so determine in your heart to take hold of victory by faith and refuse to allow yourself to be shaken and moved when some of your friends fail to recognize or understand the new you. This is to be expected because you no longer look and act like the person you used to be. There is now an aura about you, an overflowing of the anointing of the Holy Spirit (1 John 2:27). You are different because your mind has been renewed and continues to be renewed by the Word of God. "For as he thinks within himself, so he is" (Proverbs 23:7).

In closing, let's look at the words of Jesus concerning your marvelous future: "No one, after putting his hand to the plow and looking back, is fit for the kingdom of God" (Luke 9:62).

What is the Lord saying? He is saying that you, dear child of God, have entered into His Kingdom by the placing of your faith in His Son, Jesus Christ, and He doesn't want you looking back at your past failures or returning to the place where you put your trust in the Law and dead works of the Old Covenant. He wants you to keep your eyes on Him and His Kingdom as you travel the roads of life, not the rearview mirror.

I have enjoyed taking this journey with you, and I trust in the Lord that you have enjoyed it as well. Now it's time for you to flip the switch and daily, moment by moment, enjoy the unconditional love and power that resides in you. Enjoy life, and enjoy your marriage. Smile a lot, laugh a lot, be an encourager, and people will be drawn to you for the sake of the Kingdom. You are a champion and more than an overcomer through Christ Jesus. You can do it!

About The Author

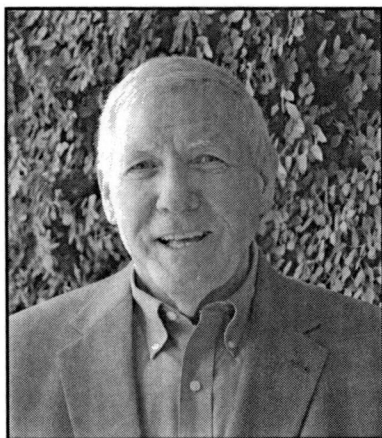

Donald Griffin

DON GRIFFIN was born in a small South Georgia town. He is a seasoned businessman with a heart for writing and teaching the Word of God. Although his parents had very little formal education, they instilled in him three very important priorities for life: the Bible, prayer, and church. As a result, he accepted Christ at the early age of twelve. At the age of seventeen, Don joined the United States Air Force with the intention of seeing the world. Instead, he was stationed in South Carolina, less than three hundred miles from his home, and stayed there until his discharge.

Don remained in South Carolina for the next ten years. During that time, he married, fathered three sons, and became a successful farmer of more than fifteen hundred acres of land. He and his family attended a small Methodist church where he taught a young couples' class and filled the pulpit when the pastor was away. Characterized by a lifestyle of seeking both the trappings of the world and the things of the Kingdom, his life began to slowly unravel. The cost was high, and at the age of thirty three, Don had lost his marriage, his sons, and his business. He decided to return to his roots in South Georgia and found the long trip back home to be one of the most lonely, heartbreaking times of his life. Back home in Georgia, Don rededicated his life to the Lord Jesus but struggled to restart his business career.

It was during this time of his life that Don met a beautiful young lady named Sarah Penny Mixon who owned and operated a very successful dance studio. Penny was also a casualty of divorce but was blessed to have exited her broken marriage with a precious daughter. They soon married, and two years later, Penny gave birth to their son.

Don continued to struggle in his efforts to establish his own business but rediscovered that God has a way of placing the right people into one's life when their trust is in Him. A successful insurance businessman came into his life and helped him establish an insurance agency of his own. Griffin Insurance Agency was born. The early years were very difficult, but Don and Penny had learned that tough times have the power to build you up or tear you down. After much prayer, Penny made a decision to leave her own business and help her husband complete his dream. Hard work and perseverance have rewarded them with a very successful Insurance Agency.

Don is now semi-retired and enjoys a great relationship

with the love of his life, Penny, and all of their children. He is a living testimony that God can take a broken life and put it back together. Don and Penny are active in their church and enjoy teaching and ministering the uncompromised Word of God into the lives of His people.

CPSIA information can be obtained at www.ICGtesting.com
Printed in the USA
LVOW10s0312060615

441456LV00003B/91/P